FIFTY-TWO YEARS IN FLORIDA.

BY JOHN C. LEY.

NASHVILLE, TENN.: DALLAS, TEX.:
PUBLISHING HOUSE OF THE M. E. CHURCH, SOUTH.
BARBEE & SMITH, AGENTS.
1899.

Notice

In many older books, foxing (or discoloration) occurs and, in some instances, print lightens with wear and age. Reprinted books, such as this, often duplicate these flaws, notwithstanding efforts to reduce or eliminate them. The pages of this reprint have been digitally enhanced and, where possible, the flaws eliminated in order to provide clarity of content and a pleasant reading experience.

Fifty-Two Years in Florida

Copyright © 1899, John C. Ley

Originally published
Nashville, Tenn. : Dallas, Tex
1899

Reprinted by:

Janaway Publishing, Inc.
732 Kelsey Ct.
Santa Maria, California 93454
(805) 925-1038
www.janawaygenealogy.com

2012

ISBN 13: 978-1-59641-260-6

The publisher gratefully acknowledges the donation of the original of this book by:

Bonita Summers, Proprietor,
Ancient City Booksellers

Made in the United States of America

TO MY BELOVED WIFE,

WHO FOR NEAR FIFTY YEARS HAS BEEN THE PARTNER
OF MY TOILS AND HOPES;

TO MY SONS,

INTO WHOSE HANDS I COMMEND THE BANNER
I MUST SOON RELEASE; AND

TO THE MEMBERS OF THE FLORIDA CONFERENCE,

WHO HAVE HONORED ME WITH A PLACE AMONG THEM,

THIS VOLUME IS DEDICATED.

PREFACE.

THE Florida Conference, at its session of January, 1885, having by resolution requested the author to write a series of articles for the *Wesleyan Christian Advocate* "with reference to their publication in a book," and recognizing that the object of said resolution was to save from oblivion some names and incidents which may in the future be useful to the Church, he did not feel at liberty to decline; and in an attempt to meet the spirit of the resolution in this humble volume has tried to give not only reminiscence, but also a brief outline of the history of the Church and State from the days of Juan Ponce de Leon to the present.

He has attempted only a connected outline, as limited space would allow no more. In doing this he lays no claim to originality, but has gathered facts from every source within reach, condensing them into as small space as possible, and presenting them in his own language. He here acknowledges obligations to Mr. Fairbanks, from whom he has drawn largely in dates and incidents.

The book as it is has commanded his earnest efforts, and as such it is commended to the Conference and public with the prayer that the critic may deal gently with an old man, whose life has been spent in talking —not writing—and begging the generous reader to remember that the preservation of facts has been his object.

CONTENTS.

PART I.

CHAPTER I.
Discovery of Florida—Juan Ponce de Leon.............. 9

CHAPTER II.
Lucas Vasquez de Ayllon—Pánfilo Narvaez—Cabeza de Vaca... 11

CHAPTER III.
Hernando de Soto....................................... 13

CHAPTER IV.
Fort Caroline—The French Massacred—Retribution..... 15

CHAPTER V.
Indians Troublesome—Treaty of 1745—Florida Ceded to Great Britain 19

PART II.

CHAPTER I.
John J. Triggs—Elijah Sinclair—Donald MacDonell—John Slade... 24

CHAPTER II.
Missions in the East—J. N. Glenn—Allen Turner—J. L. Jerry—St. Augustine.................................. 28

CHAPTER III.
Tallahassee—Josiah Evans—Adam Wyrick.............. 31

CHAPTER IV.
Extracts from the Diary of Isaac Boring............... 36

CHAPTER V.
Indian Atrocities—John L. Jerry—James B. Jackson—W. M. Crumley—R. H. Howren...................... 50

PART III.

CHAPTER I.
The Author Transferred to the Florida Conference 58

CHAPTER II.
Our First Conference and Its Members 60

CHAPTER III.
Second Conference—The Armed Occupation Act—A. J. Deavours—Extracts from Journal 64

CHAPTER IV.
Our Third Conference—Hamilton Circuit—Affliction 69

CHAPTER V.
From 1849 to 1853 72

CHAPTER VI.
From 1854 to 1858 78

CHAPTER VII.
From 1860 to 1863 84

CHAPTER VIII.
From 1863 to 1866 93

CHAPTER IX.
From 1867 to 1876 99

CHAPTER X.
From 1877 to 1880 107

CHAPTER XI.
From 1877 to 1883 111

CHAPTER XII.
From 1884 to 1889 114

CHAPTER XIII.
From 1888 to 1895 119

CHAPTER XIV.
Conclusion 126

APPENDIX.
Centenary of Methodism 133
A Sermon 146

PART I.

CHAPTER I.

Discovery of Florida—Juan Ponce de Leon.

IN attempting to trace a brief outline of Florida's early history we meet at every step the most serious difficulties. We are carried back to the days of romance and chivalry, long before any other settlements were made in the wilds of America.

The character and objects of the explorers, the ferocity and cruelty of the natives, throw around chivalry and heroism the horrors of deception and carnage. The first, and perhaps the most important, of these explorers was Juan Ponce de Leon. He was a companion of Columbus in his second voyage to America, afterwards he held an office under Orvando in Hispaniola. Under orders from Spain he visited and conquered Porto Rico. He had heard of a famous country lying to the northwest, possessing all the charms of an El Dorado, and also of a fountain capable of affording perpetual youth. Having acquired considerable wealth and having been supplanted as governor of Porto Rico, in the spring of 1512 he fitted out an expedition of three vessels, left Hispaniola, and landed near where St. Augustine now stands, on Palm Sunday. It being the day for church decorations, the wild luxuriance of flowers naturally suggested the name of Florida for the country.

Ponce de Leon's first object was to obtain gold and precious stones. These he obtained not. He sought the fountain of youth. This he found not. The author of these lines, after over three hundred and fifty years from that time, having floated upon the waters of Silver Spring, Crystal River, and other enchanting streams of beauty in Florida; having bathed in her fountains and eaten her golden fruit, feels that Ponce de Leon's fountain was within the reach of fancy, though not of fact.

But Ponce de Leon came not to develop the country, but to obtain what he could from it. Thus disappointed, he returned to Spain, making, however, a favorable report.

In 1521 he returned as adelantado (governor) of Florida, or Bimini. He made proclamation of his adelantadoship, and demanded allegiance from the natives. But the answer was by no means satisfactory, for the natives fiercely attacked his forces, killing many of his troops and sorely wounding the governor.

Thus wounded in body, and sorely crushed in spirit, Ponce de Leon returned to Cuba, where after a few days he died. His gubernatorial honors were to him sad failures. Instead of obtaining gold and precious stones, he squandered his own vast wealth. His El Dorado was a barren waste. Instead of finding a fountain of youth, the fountain of his life passed away. His brief epitaph reads in Spanish: "In this sepulcher rest the bones of a man who was a *Lion* by name and still more by nature."

CHAPTER II.

Lucas Vasquez de Ayllon—Pánfilo Narvaez—Cabeza de Vaca.

AMONG the early adventurers who came to Florida was Lucas Vasquez de Ayllon. He was an officer of some distinction in Hispaniola. With six of his neighbors, he fitted out an expedition in 1520 for the purpose of procuring laborers. They landed at various points, receiving only kindness from the natives. By gifts and protestations of friendship he finally induced about one hundred and thirty to go aboard his vessels, and immediately struck sail for Hispaniola. One of his vessels foundered at sea, and all aboard went down. The other reached its destination; but the proud spirit of the Indians could not brook their fearful lot, and we are told that "these Indians profited them nothing, because they all died of care and grief."

Not discouraged by the fruitless attempt, he again returned to Florida, in 1524, with three vessels. The Indians received them with every mark of friendship, until all fears were allayed. They then attacked them so vigorously that nearly the whole expedition was massacred, Vasquez de Ayllon perishing in the havoc. We cannot follow the various expeditions nor notice the duplicity, sufferings, and heroism of the Spaniards on the one hand, and the cunning, bloodthirsty spirit of the Indians on the other. This one adventure, with a change of names, numbers, and incidents, is a clear representation of nearly all.

But we must not pass unnoticed the expedition of

Pánfilo Narvaez, who left Spain in 1527 with five vessels and six hundred men. Stopping at Hispaniola, one hundred and forty of his men withdrew. In April, 1528, he reëmbarked with four hundred men and eighty horses. On the 15th of April he anchored in what is supposed to be Tampa Bay. The following day he took formal possession of the country in the name of the king of Spain. One hundred men remained with the vessels; and three hundred men, with forty horses (all that survived the voyage), undertook to make their way through the country. They met the fiercest opposition from the natives, and, worn by hunger, disease, and savage warfare, they pursued a northerly course, crossing the Withlacoochee and Suwannee Rivers. The survivors at last reached either St. Mark's or Apalachee Bay. Here they constructed rude boats and all of them but four went aboard and attempted to make their way to the coast of Mexico. After untold perils, hardships, and hunger, the last of them perished on Mobile Bay.

Cabeza de Vaca, with three others, refused to go aboard, went to the Indians and presented themselves as great "medicine men," and were spared. After seven years they succeeded in making their way westward, crossed the Mississippi River, and finally, meeting a party of Spaniards from Mexico, escaped and reached Spain.

"To De Soto is ascribed the discovery of the Mississippi, but Cabeza de Vaca and his companions had rested upon its banks before De Soto left Spain." (Fairbanks.)

CHAPTER III.

Hernando de Soto.

AMONG the Spanish cavaliers who undertook the conquest of Florida none occupies the prominence of Hernando de Soto. At an early age he went out under Don Pedro Arias de Avila, then governor of the West Indies, who placed him in command of a troop of horsemen.

In 1531 he was dispatched with one hundred men and a supply of horses to join Pizarro against Peru. He became a valuable auxiliary to Pizarro, rose rapidly, soon became second in command, and with a small force captured the Inca.

To avoid disagreement between the leaders, he took his share of the vast booty and returned to Spain in 1536. The laurels already won, and his great wealth and influence with the Spanish court, could not satisfy his restless and daring spirit. He undertook the conquest of Florida. Having received from Spain the title "Governor of Cuba and Florida, and marquis of all the lands he might conquer," he landed at Tampa Bay May 25, 1539, with about one thousand men and three hundred and fifty horses. They soon began their northerly march, passing, as nearly as can now be ascertained, close by where Ocala now stands; thence northwest, to the region of Tallahassee; thence northeast, crossing the Altamaha; thence, pursuing a westerly direction, passing near the present site of Rome, Ga., and crossing the Mississippi about Memphis. Such a journey, with no supplies but such as could be secured from savage foes, and especially through an altogether unknown country, as far as we know, has no parallel in history.

It was his intention to pursue a southwesterly course from thence into Mexico. Soon after crossing the river they met insurmountable difficulties. Disease arrested the commander, who, after making the best arrangements he could for his followers, died May 21, 1542, having spent about three years in his explorations. His followers buried him in the river, and, having constructed rude boats, they descended the river to its mouth, thence coasted westerly until they reached the Spaniards in Mexico.

CHAPTER IV.

Fort Caroline—The French Massacred—Retribution.

HITHERTO we have followed the Cavalier, whose object was glory and spoils, but we now come to a different class of emigrants. At this time Europe was in a state of war between the Romanists and Protestants. Charles IX. was king of France, and Coligny was head of the Protestant party. An expedition was fitted out by the latter, for the purpose of extending the possessions of France, and at the same time, in case of reverses at home, to provide an asylum for the Huguenots. The expedition consisted of two vessels, and sailed in 1562, under Jean Ribault. A prosperous voyage brought them to Florida, near St. Augustine. Sailing northward, they landed at the mouth of St. John's River and erected a monument of stone having on it the French coat of arms. Again sailing northward, they reached Port Royal, S. C., where they left a colony of twenty-five men. Ribault returned to France for supplies and reënforcements, but, owing to the fierceness of the civil war then raging, he was unable to do anything for his settlement in America. His little colony waited long for his return, and at last, in despair, constructed a rude vessel and attempted to return to France, and were finally rescued by an English vessel.

After the truce in France, Coligny turned his attention to America, and fitted out an expedition under René de Laudonnière, who had accompanied Ribault. They reached shore June 22, 1564. The description of their landing place corresponds to that of St. Augustine. The next day they sailed north and settled at what is known as St. John's Bluff. Here they built a fort, which they called Fort Caroline.

A fleet of seven vessels was sent May 17, 1565, for the relief of the fort. Menendez set sail from Spain July 1, and reached St. Augustine August 29, the same day that the French cast anchor at the mouth of the St. John's. The Spaniards learning through the Indians the position of the French, a council of war was called. The officers generally were in favor of returning to Hispaniola and making preparations to attack the French in the spring, but Menendez could brook no delay and resolved to attack them at once. Preparations were made accordingly, and about daybreak the Spanish vessels began moving toward the French transports. These, fearing the design of the Spaniards, slipped anchors and put out to sea. The Spaniards, seeing them, fired their heaviest guns, but at too great distance for effect. Pursuit was kept up all day, and, failing to overtake them, they returned at night. Ribault watched their movements, and at once resolved to make an attempt to surprise them. Accordingly on the 8th of September he reëmbarked with most of his able-bodied men, leaving Laudonnière with an invalid force to defend Fort Caroline.

Two days afterwards Ribault encountered a fearful gale, which drove him helplessly before it and stranded his vessels on the beach south of St. Augustine. In the meantime Menendez determined to make a prompt attack upon Fort Caroline. His force was about six hundred, and he supposed that of the French about the same, or perhaps a little more.

Having obtained guides, he resolved, against the advice of his officers, to move forward at once, especially as the raging storm seemed to favor his design of surprising the French. Accordingly, on the 17th of September, at the head of five hundred men, he reached the vicinity of the fort. Laudonnière had done all he could to repair the fort, but he was sick himself, and had only about sixteen well men in his command. The night of the 19th was stormy, and at dawn the sentinels were withdrawn under shelter. Soon after, Menendez reached the fort and commenced the attack, there was a sudden rush, a feeble resistance, and the fort was taken; the garrison was cut down without regard to age or sex; the captives were hung upon the neighboring trees, and an inscription in Spanish was placed over them: "I do this not as to Frenchmen, but as to Lutherans."

Menendez changed the name of the fort to San Mateo, whose festival occurred the next day. His return to St. Augustine was signalized with great rejoicing, a solemn mass and *Te Deum* in honor of the victory.

The news of the disaster to Ribault's vessels was carried to St. Augustine by Indians, and Menendez set out with a party of his men and reached Matanzas inlet that night. In the morning he saw a number of men on the opposite shore. One of them swam over and informed them that they were Frenchmen under the command of Ribault, whose vessels had been wrecked. He demanded an unconditional surrender, and brought them over ten at a time, marched them out of sight of their comrades, and had them put to death.

The Spanish court rejoiced greatly over the victory. The pope sent Menendez a congratulatory letter, and the French court, in consequence of religious animosities, received the news with perfect indifference. Menendez now applied himself zealously in strengthening his forts and looking after his missions.

Although the French court treated this outrage with indifference, the people did not; and one Dominique de Gourgues fitted an expedition and obtained a license for a voyage to Africa to purchase slaves. After passing San Domingo, he revealed to his followers his true design, which they received gladly. On approaching the shore the Indians menaced his landing with great bitterness; but learning that they were Frenchmen, and enemies to the Spaniards, they welcomed them to the shore, and brought their warriors to aid them.

De Gourges surprised and captured the fort, and upon the same trees upon which the Frenchmen had been hung he hanged their executioners, and in the same place where Menendez had raised his inscription, "I do this, not as unto Frenchmen, but as unto Lutherans," De Gourges engraved on a pine board with a red-hot iron: "I do this not as unto Spaniards, but as unto traitors, thieves, and murderers." De Gourges, after returning thanks to God, went back to France, arriving in La Rochelle June 6, 1568.

CHAPTER V.

Indians Troublesome--Treaty of 1745—Florida Ceded to Great Britain.

MENENDEZ had established his settlement at St. Augustine, destroyed the French settlement at Fort Caroline, and returned to Spain. He was at Madrid when De Gourges so fearfully avenged the tragedy at Fort Caroline. He returned with funds and reënforcements for the further amplifying of his plans. He brought missionaries for the conversion of the Indians, and immediately began to strengthen his defenses, and plant outposts and missions, at various points along the St. John's River and the Atlantic coast. Five years after this the son of a chief became dissatisfied with the restraints and reproofs of the priest, and formed a conspiracy for the destruction of all the priests and mission stations of the colony. The utmost savage ferocity and cruelty followed. Its details can be found in any of the histories of Florida. But we are not inclined to follow the bloody recitals; suffice it to say, no station outside of St. Augustine escaped. Some of the priests were slain in their robes before their altars.

From this time English settlements had been formed at Jamestown, Va., and the Carolinas and at Savannah, Ga. Jealousy of territorial rights, antipathy of nationality, with the bloodthirsty spirit of the savages, who were always ready to aid one party in the destruction of another, kept up a chronic war, savage in spirit and bloody in detail. But the design of this work will not allow us to follow them farther.

A treaty was concluded in 1745, between Great Britain and Spain, by which hostilities between the colonies were suspended, but they were renewed in 1762, and Havana fell into the hands of the English. A treaty was finally concluded in 1763, by which Cuba was restored to Spain, and Florida was ceded to Great Britain. By treaty stipulation free toleration was granted to the Catholics in Florida.

The policy of the English was very liberal to settlers. At the time of the change of flags the Spanish flag had floated over St. Augustine for one hundred and ninety years, but, with the exception of a few military and mission stations, the country was but little better known than in the days of De Leon. But liberal government, fertile soil, and genial climate made rapid development of her resources.

During our Revolutionary struggle Florida assumed considerable importance. The policy of Great Britain had been liberal to her, the citizens had just commenced developing their resources, and with almost unanimity were loyal to the crown. Loyalists from the southern colonies fled to her as a rendezvous. To the British it was of incalculable importance; the strong fort at St. Augustine served them for a prison; predatory bands crossed the river and laid waste the country, carrying off provisions and slaves. The Indians also became an important factor in the struggle; but the war finally closed, and, in 1783, Florida was receded to Spain without the treaty stipulation of religious toleration, which she had demanded of Great Britain for Catholics. No tongue or pen can describe the sad disappointment of the settlers upon the change of flags. All progress was arrested. For twenty years every encouragement had been extended to immigrants, and thousands had flocked in, built houses, opened farms, planted gardens, and were just beginning to extend to the markets of the world specimens of her golden fruits. But the change of government, policy, and religion paralyzed everything. Those who had left the colonies before the war could return, but the wounds were too fresh for those who had deserted them during that fearful struggle, and had identified themselves with their enemies, to find a welcome in the homes they had left.

To every English and American settler, with but very few exceptions, a move was necessary. After the English and American settlers had left Florida the development was slow. The contracted policy of the government, and the hostility of the Indians, rendered progress impossible.

Things continued in this state till near the opening of the war with Great Britain in 1812. As the prospects of the war became imminent it was supposed that Great Britain would seize Florida. To forestall that move, commissioners were sent by the United States to make stipulations for the occupancy of the territory, and, in case of failure of negotiations, should there be room to entertain a suspicion that a design existed on the part of any other power to occupy Florida, they were authorized to take possession of the province with the forces of the United States. The Spanish government refused to surrender her province, and in the spring of 1812 settlers from between the St. John's and St. Mary's Rivers, with numbers from Georgia, organized in the name of Patriots. Gen. J. H. McIntosh was elected governor of the "Republic of Florida," and on the 17th of March captured Fernandina. Although the government of the United States did not acknowledge the acts of her agents, yet her troops occupied portions of the territory for several years, during which time they conducted sanguinary wars with the Indians, especially in Alachua against King Philip and Billy Bowlegs.

In August, 1814, the British occupied Pensacola, and Gen. Andrew Jackson was sent to dislodge them. He sent forward a flag of truce, which was fired upon, whereupon he took the town and fort by storm. The British and Indians escaped to their vessels. Jackson blew up their forts and marched to New Orleans. Col. Nichols, having been expelled from Pensacola, devoted his attention to forming an Indian and negro rendezvous upon the Appalachicola River. A fort was built of massive walls, heavy cannon were mounted, and the garrison was well armed. They were protected by the river in front, a dense swamp in the rear, and a creek above and below. It was garrisoned with three hundred British troops, a large number of Indians, and also a large number of negroes, who had escaped from the States. After the war was over the British troops were withdrawn, leaving the fort and defenses in the hands of the Indians and negroes. In 1816 Col. Clinch reduced this fort and returned the negroes to their owners.

Instigated by the British, the Seminole Indians, with the aid of other small tribes, kept up an almost unceasing predatory war with the whites bordering on Florida. In January, 1818, Gen. Jackson concluded a treaty of peace with the Creeks, and engaged them to aid him against the Seminoles. The following spring, with five hundred regulars, one thousand militia, and about two thousand Indians, he marched into Florida. At Miccosukee he routed the Indians, and found some three hundred scalps of men, women, and children, mostly fresh, which had recently been exhibited to grace their triumph. From thence he marched to Fowlstown, where he met but feeble resistance; from thence to St. Mark's, which was strongly fortified and had twenty guns. The fort surrendered without resistance. The prophet Francis and another chief were captured and hanged. From St. Marks he marched to Suwannee, where he dispersed a large force and took many prisoners. Among the latter were two Englishmen, Arbuthnot and Ambrister. They were tried by court-martial for furnishing the Indians arms and ammunition, were found guilty, and executed. This for a time so humbled the Indians that the settlers enjoyed peace.

PART II.

CHAPTER I.

John J. Triggs—Elijah Sinclair—Donald MacDonell—John Slade.

On the 22d of February, 1819, a treaty was concluded between Spain and the United States, in which Florida was ceded to the latter. This was ratified February 19, 1821, and the change of flags took place the same year, at St. Augustine July 10, and at Pensacola July 21. From that time it was under military control until March 3, 1822, when, by an act of Congress, it was organized into a territorial government.

Soon after the exchange of flags population commenced flowing rapidly into the Territory. The fertility of the soil and salubrity of the climate called loudly for population, and the response was prompt. The Indians were scattered all over the country, and looked with extreme jealousy upon all encroachments on the part of the whites; while the latter had no idea of leaving the vast and fertile lands to a few thousand Indians for hunting grounds.

Soon after immigration began we find the missionary in various places, but so brief and disconnected are the notices that we have been unable to gather the names and dates of their labors, so as to present them in anything like connected form. In 1821 John J. Triggs was sent to a new mission called Alapaha (printed in Minutes Lapaha). It extended from the Ocmulgee to the Florida line, and, from the testimony of old settlers, he extended his labors into Florida, and he was, from all that I can gather, the first Protestant minister that ever preached in the Territory, unless it may have been during the English occupancy of the same. Mr. Triggs was an Englishman by birth, a strong reasoner, and a thorough Methodist, ever ready to defend the doctrines of his Church, and often in sarcastic language. He finally located, and spent his last years in Burke County, Ga., an honored and useful local preacher. His name was often spoken of with highest respect during my first years in the State.

Elijah Sinclair was appointed in 1822 to St. Mary's and Amelia Island. During the war of 1812 Fernandina had attained considerable importance. Being the northeast corner of Florida and a fine harbor, it became a center for exchange of contraband goods. I have heard my father-in-law, John Pottle, say that he had seen some hundreds of vessels in that port at once. After the war it declined in importance. Still for years there was a slave mart, and a considerable town there; but when the author served St. Mary's, in 1848, the town consisted of a few families who kept the lighthouse.

After the purchase of Yellow Bluff by the Florida Railroad Company and the locating of the eastern terminus of the railroad there, it again came into importance and has continued to improve, though its development has not kept pace with the expectations of its friends. Here Mr. Sinclair found a few sympathizers, among them Donald MacDonell, who was one of the first fruits of Methodism in the State. His house was the home and preaching place of the young itinerant. He left a large family, whose descendants fill many important positions both in Florida and Georgia. We might also name Mr. Seaton, who gave the young preacher a welcome. Smith says: "We may safely say that the first Protestant preaching in Florida was on Amelia Island." Yet the same year (1822) Mr. Triggs was sent to organize a mission in Southwest Georgia. This mission embraced parts of Georgia, Alabama, and Florida, to say nothing of his work the previous year on Alapaha Mission, which doubtless extended into Middle Florida. Be that as it may, we know that in 1822 the gospel was preached by Methodist itinerants in Florida, both east and west of the Suwannee River.

In 1823 John Slade was sent as junior preacher with Mr. Triggs to the mission formed the previous year. Though not the first, he was among the first preachers who brought the gospel into the Territory of Florida, and from his continued connection with the country, and his great success as a pioneer, he has been called the "Father of Methodism in Florida." He traveled one year, and then began his regular itinerant career on the Chattahoochee Mission. He traveled several years and then located, giving much useful labor to the Church. He was readmitted at Tallahassee in 1845, when our Conference was organized. Here I first met him. His locks were white; he was tall, straight, and commanding in appearance; a powerful voice, though somewhat cracked by overstraining. He preached from a heart overflowing with love. To him the cross, heaven, and hell were awful realities, and while he preached sinners trembled. The chief source of his power, under the Holy Ghost, was his own deep conviction of the awful truths he uttered. He continued a faithful and useful member of the Conference, till called to his reward in 1854.

CHAPTER II.

Missions in the East—J. N. Glenn—Allen Turner—J. L. Jerry —St. Augustine.

WHILE Triggs and Slade carried the gospel to the pioneers in the West J. N. Glenn was sent to St. Augustine. He was the first missionary whose work lay entirely in Florida. During the Spanish occupancy Protestants had been excluded, but now that it was open to them our Church was prompt to enter the open door.

Mr. Glenn found only one member of his church in the "Ancient City," but succeeded during the year in organizing a society of ten members.

Allen Turner was presiding elder of Oconee District, which extended into Florida. "He held a quarterly meeting in St. Augustine, the first ever held in our Territory. We are told that forty-two persons knelt at the communion. A church was finally built in the city, and for some years had a feeble existence; but after the growth at Jacksonville and the opening of interior towns it was abandoned." (Smith). The communicants referred to above were doubtless chiefly blacks. Methodism, from the first, in that place was successful with them; but the whites, nearly all being Minorcans and Roman Catholics, were inaccessible. The society of blacks maintained their existence until the mission was renewed by our Conference in 1845.

I do not know the year, probably 1823 or 1824, when John L. Jerry was sent to St. Augustine, but from hearing him often speak of it I know it was not long after the change of flags. He was a native of North Carolina; born May 11, 1793. In 1818 he was admitted into the South Carolina Conference, and was one of the early missionaries sent to Florida. I know not the bounds of his work, but know from his own lips that it embraced St. Augustine, Cowford (Jacksonville), Fernandina, Newnansville, and Micanopy. The character of the work may be inferred by one or two incidents which I have heard him relate.

In St. Augustine the population was nearly all Catholics. Soon after he began preaching there the priest met him, and after some violence of language absolutely forbade his preaching in the city. Mr. Jerry simply pointed to the stars and stripes floating from the top of the fort, and said: "No Inquisition where that flag floats." His society of blacks still exists, though at the close of the war they went to the Methodist Episcopal Church.

From St. Augustine to Cowford (Jacksonville), forty miles, he traveled without seeing a house; from thence to Newnansville, sixty-five miles, by Indian trail; thence to Micanopy, thirty miles, etc. These lonely rides the missionary made on horseback, carrying his clothes, books, lunch, and a little sack of corn to feed his horse. He told me that during one of these lonely rides, his money reduced to less than one dollar, he stopped to lunch and feed his horse. Feeling deeply depressed, he went to a cluster of bushes to pray. Seeing something glitter in the sunshine and supposing it was a button dropped by some Cavalier of the olden time, he thought he would go and pick it up as a relic. But what was his surprise when, on taking it in his hand, he found it a Spanish doubloon ($16). This met all his wants until Quarterly Conference, when he received his installment of missionary money. Beyond this, it established in his mind that faith in God's special promises which he never lost.

During the darkest days of the Indian war he went from post to post preaching the gospel, and, although massacres were frequent around him, he was never disturbed. He remarked to me: "The people say the reason I was not troubled was because the Indians knew me, but I say God protected me."

In 1836 he was on the Tallahassee District. At the organization of our Conference he was in the local ranks, but was readmitted at Monticello in 1846, and filled many of our most important places until, in 1859, in holy triumph he passed to his reward.

CHAPTER III.

Tallahassee—Josiah Evans—Adam Wyrick.

IN 1824 Florida was made a district, and Josiah Evans was appointed presiding elder. The immigration to Middle Florida had been so rapid that the Indians had retired to the east and south of the Suwannee. The influx of population had been phenomenal. Tallahassee, its capital, was rapidly becoming a center of wealth, fashion, and refinement. Mr. Evans was a man of rather rough exterior, yet dauntless, energetic, and spiritual. He presided over the district, and was nobly sustained by such men as Morgan C. Turrentine, John L. Jerry, with other itinerant and local preachers, the laymen giving efficient aid. It was a year of great prosperity, and five hundred and seventeen whites and one hundred and seven blacks were reported from the district that year.

In 1825 a church was built in Tallahassee. Josiah Evans was still presiding elder. The builder was Rev. C. Woodbury, the father of Rev. S. Woodbury, of our Conference. The house was a plain wooden structure without ceiling, paint, sash, or blinds; but board shutters supplied their places, and for many years this building served the people for a place of worship, and, as far as I know, was the first Methodist church built in Florida. I have been unable to obtain the names of the missionaries for this year, but Chattahoochee and St. Augustine were among the appointments. The country around Tallahassee was filling up, and doubtless some of the local preachers who made their mark in early Methodism in the State were here at that time, though we can only speak for certain of Mr. Woodbury. We have found but meager reports of the work in 1825; but, as seen above, Josiah Evans still filled the Tallahassee District, Chattahoochee being served by Elisha Callaway and Jesse Boring.

We have been unable to procure any *data* of the work in 1826 and 1827; but in 1828 Tallahassee was made a station, it having been served previously as one of the appointments of a circuit, Josiah Evans, presiding elder, and Josiah Freeman, preacher in charge.

Smith says: "The Florida work still went on in the midst of difficulties. A body of settlers had settled on Pea River, in the west of Florida, and a camp meeting was held there. Although there were not more than one hundred and fifty people present, there were twenty-seven conversions. In the far west of Florida, at Homes Valley Mission, there was also a successful work."

Adam Wyrick and D. MacDonell were on the Leon Circuit, which included Leon, Jefferson, Madison, and Gadsden Counties, extending from the Apalachicola to the Suwannee River, and from Georgia to the Gulf. Mr. Wyrick traveled on horseback through the country from Monroe Circuit, Georgia, to reach this work. He was a man of great physical power, intellectual, earnest, and practical. I do not know what year he located, but when I came to Florida he was an honored local preacher. My first night in Monticello was spent at his house. He loved the preachers, loved to talk of the early days of the itinerant in Florida. He was a ripe counselor and a fast friend. He lived to very great age, and died in peace a few years since. Isaac Boring was moved from Keowee Circuit, South Carolina, to Pensacola, Fla. There was general prosperity reported from the Territory this year, with an increase of three hundred and fourteen members.

In 1829 Z. Dowling was sent as presiding elder to the Tallahassee District, where he remained four years, John D. Bowen, preacher in charge. They had a year of prosperity: thirty-five white and twenty-four colored members were added to the Church. John F. Weathersby traveled in the eastern part of the State, where, Smith tells us: "A pole cabin with dirt floor, was his resting place, and a ride of twenty-five miles, through an untracked wild, was needful to reach a congregation of half a dozen hearers. This was his daily work."

In 1830 Isaac Boring served Tallahassee Station, and John W. Talley, Pensacola. I will here give a few reminiscences of Talley, as recorded by Smith, to illustrate the life of the missionaries to Florida in those days: "He left Columbia, S. C., on horseback, spent a few days in Greene County (Georgia), and rode through the State to Columbus. Here he purchased a sulky, but his horse, taking fright at a thunder storm, ran away, broke the sulky to pieces, and though he was only badly bruised he narrowly escaped death. He then refitted and turned to the south. He was now in the Indian Nation. He reached a white settlement in Henry County, Ala., the next day. Making his way through the flat woods of Eastern and Southern Alabama, he pressed on. Houses were few and accommodations poor indeed. At a little log cabin, the home of a hunter, he was sheltered for the night, and fed upon musty corn bread, the meal beaten in a mortar, and the tough lungs of a deer fried in rancid bacon grease, and corn coffee, sweetened with sirup. On such fare the missionary could not break his long fast, and it was fifteen miles to the next house. He found, however, an oasis in the desert (a widow's neat cottage and well-supplied table). Thence he pushed through the rain, to the house of the first Methodist he had seen since leaving Columbus. After reaching the Florida sea-coast, and crossing Escambia Bay, he found himself still ten miles from Pensacola, and with no choice but to walk. He began bravely enough, but soon his limbs gave out. He reached the city, however, the next day."

We have been unable to procure the minutes of the Conferences prior to 1846; hence the works, who served them, and when, especially in the eastern part of our territory, we have to leave for revelation before the great white throne. A published sermon of Rev. E. L. T. Blake, preached upon the fiftieth anniversary of that church, has given us much information upon which we have drawn.

We know that John L. Jerry had married and settled his family near the Suwannee, and devoted his wonderful energies to his Master's cause, a large part of his time being given to the east.

James Hutto was also a pioneer in that section, whose name was precious among the people when I first came to this country. Among the local preachers were "Uncle Dick" and Thomas Taylor, with others of precious memory. "Uncle Dick" Taylor was a man of wonderful unction; his whole soul seemed to be in his work, and perhaps few in his day were honored with more conversions to Christ than he.

CHAPTER IV.

Extracts from the Diary of Isaac Boring.

I WILL here favor the reader with some extracts from the diary of Rev. Isaac Boring, as published by his son, Rev. I. W. Boring, in the *Florida Christian Advocate:*

DIARY.

On Monday, the 28th of January, 1828, I left my father's house for the seat of the South Carolina Conference, held at Camden, S. C. The mode of travel was horseback. Starting from Jackson County, Ga., I arrived at Camden February 6; was appointed to the Pensacola Mission February 14; set out for my appointment; went via Augusta, Macon, and Columbus, Ga.; crossed the Chattahoochee River at Marshall's Ferry; traveled thirty-three miles, which brought me to the Creek Nation on Wednesday, 5th of March; rode forty miles to the Choctawhatchee settlement.

On Wednesday, March 12, 1828, I reached Pensacola. I find by counting the distance traveled each day that I have ridden six hundred and twenty miles since I left Camden. Brother Hardy is in Pensacola, and intended to leave to-morrow, but he has concluded to wait another day, to give me an introduction to the people, and necessary instructions about the work.

On Friday, March 14, Brother Hardy leaves Pensacola, and takes my horse at one hundred dollars. I find that we have no place of worship here, but use the courthouse. I have boarded with Dr. Fanda since I arrived here.

On March 19th I rode to Mr. Bamans', and preached in his schoolhouse to a small congregation.

On the 21st I preached at Mr. Gains's. Here we have a small society.

On the 25th I returned to Pensacola and commenced to board with Brother Hannah at $12 per month.

On the 2d of May Brother Josiah Evans, the presiding elder, arrived, and held our Quarterly Conference.

On the 19th of June I left Brother Hannah, and moved into a small house in the lower part of town. I am not pleased with my situation. I feel very unwilling to live by myself so far from any family. I have sought in vain to get board with a private family in this place; only at Brother Hannah's, and it is not practicable for me to board there at present. I often think of my father's house; I know I could find a lodging place there; but I am far away from home and among strangers, and some who appear to be unfriendly toward me. But I remember that my Master before me had not where to lay his head. I am better treated than he was. I have sinned against God and deserve punishment, but Jesus never sinned.

On Sunday, June 22, for the first time the citizens of Pensacola met in the Methodist Episcopal Church, to worship the God of heaven. At nine o'clock Sabbath school commenced; at half-past ten I preached from the Psalm cxxii., first verse: "I was glad when they said unto me, Let us go into the house of the Lord." At 4 P.M. I preached to the colored people from 1 Peter v. 6: "Humble yourselves therefore under the mighty hand of God, that he may exalt you in due time." I preached at night from Proverbs viii. 35, 36.

On Thursday, the 26th, I rode out to the cantonment and preached to the soldiers.

On the 1st of July I moved to Dr. Fanday's, where I expect to reside during my stay in Pensacola.

On Thursday, the 26th, I rode to Mr. Eubanks'. Only two persons beside the family met. I gave a short talk. Mr. Eubanks wrote me a letter, informing me that he was unwilling to have preaching any longer in his house; so I left no appointment. After the meeting closed I rode to Black Creek, and preached the next day.

On Saturday, the 28th, I preached at John's; rode in the evening to Mr. Ward's and spent the night.

On Sunday, the 29th, my horse had to swim the Santa Fé Creek; I was carried over on a raft. I then rode to Rocky Creek and swam my horse, riding him. I got wet, but received no injury. I soon got to Dell's Meetinghouse and preached. After service went to Maxy Dell's.

On Monday, the 30th, I rode to Mr. Burnett's and preached. I spoke with liberty and plainness.

On Tuesday, the 31st, I preached near Mrs. Love's in an old dwelling they have fixed up for divine services.

On Wednesday, April 1st, I preached at Wanton's.

On Thursday, the 2d, I rode to Palatka [spelled in the diary, Paladkey].

On Friday, the 3d, I crossed the river; preached at Brother Rushe's to a few persons.

On Saturday, the 4th, I rode to town [St. Augustine], and found that Brother Evans, the presiding elder, had preached in the morning.

I preached again on Sunday, and administered the sacrament of the Lord's Supper; the Presbyterian minister communed with us, but the Episcopalian minister did not.

On Tuesday night, at the request of Mr. Ball, I met a few colored persons in a small meetinghouse of many years' standing, which has been occupied by a small society of colored Baptists.

On Wednesday evening, at the request of Mr. Ball, I held a meeting with a few soldiers.

On Friday, the 10th, I fasted and prayed; at night met the Methodist class and examined all the members present. We had the good Spirit with us.

On Sunday, the 12th, at 11 A.M., I heard Mr. Alexander, of the Presbyterian Church, preach; I preached at night.

On Sunday, the 19th, I preached in Jacksonville, filling all the appointments of the week; in the evening I set out for Brother Nelson's, but got lost, and found myself near Mr. Eubanks'. It was then dark and I was about four miles from Brother Nelson's. I concluded I would try to reach his house. I started and got about one mile; my horse left the road, and I could not see the place. I got off my horse and got upon my knees and prayed for direction. I concluded to try and get back to Mr. Eubanks'. I succeeded, and the family appeared to receive me kindly. I had better liberty to talk that night with the family.

On Monday I rode to Mr. Gary's, where I was kindly entertained by the family during my stay.

On Tuesday, the 21st, I rode to Brother Phillips' and preached.

On Wednesday, the 22d, I rode to Mr. Johns's with the expectation of preaching, but was disappointed in a congregation. The people in this settlement generally call themselves Baptists, and do not care to hear the Methodists preach. I read a chapter, sang a hymn, prayed, and closed the meeting. I told them I would not have another opportunity until they were more anxious to hear preaching. In the afternoon I rode to Mr. Ward's and found about one dozen persons present waiting to hear me preach. I did so, and left an appointment for my next round at Mr. Carter's, in the same settlement. I hope the Lord intends to raise himself up a people in this place.

On Thursday, the 23d, I preached at Dell's Meetinghouse. (Appointments all filled.)

On Thursday, the 30th, I set out early in the morning for St. Augustine. I took a wrong road, and after traveling over it for some time I left it and wandered through the woods and through a very bad thicket, and got back to the St. John's River after traveling for three hours and a quarter. When I got to the river I could not tell whether I was above or below Palatka, and of course could not tell what direction I ought to pursue. I got off my horse and got upon my knees and tried to lay my case before the Lord and ask for the guidance of his Spirit. When I arose and got up on my horse I came to the conclusion that I was below Palatka. I traveled accordingly, and soon got on the right road, and felt that the good Lord had heard my prayer and set me aright. Late in the evening I got to St. Augustine, and put up at Brother Davis'.

On Sunday, May 3, I preached at the Government House. I announced that I would preach the next Sabbath in the Methodist church now building.

On Tuesday evening I met the class.

On Saturday, the 9th, I attended court in order to hear law points argued by Mr. Willis, of Georgia.

On Sunday, May 10, 1829, I commenced divine service in the Methodist Episcopal Church. The congregation was good. My text was Matthew xxi., first part of the 13th verse. I was about the middle of my discourse when a fire broke out near the church. The people left the church to put out the fire. They soon returned, and I finished my discourse. Preached again in the evening; text, Matthew xxi. 24. Preached again at night from 1 Samuel xii. 24, 25. I spoke with considerable liberty. This closed the labors of the day, after dedicating the first Protestant church that was ever built in St. Augustine, the oldest town in the United States. I humbly hope the Lord will accept the house, and honor it with the conversion of many souls.

On Sunday, the 17th, I preached in Jacksonville. For the first time, I was allowed to preach in the courthouse. [He does not state in what house he had preached before this.] During divine service a drunken man made so much noise that Mr. Hart very politely led him out of the house. After preaching I met the society, filling all the appointments of the week.

On Sunday, the 24th, I preached at Mrs. Louis'.

On Monday, the 25th, I preached at Wanton's, after which I rode twenty-five miles to the Seminole

Agency. While riding through the rain and dark, with no human being with me, my soul was comforted on the reflection of the omnipresence of my Saviour; I felt he was near to bless and preserve me.

On Tuesday, the 26th, I visited Camp King [I learn it is a few miles west of Ocala] with an intention to ask leave to preach to the soldiers. There were but a few present, and they were at work. I therefore did not think it wise under the circumstances to ask permission. I asked the commanding officer if it would be agreeable to have preaching among his men. He said it would be on the Sabbath day, and requested me to call when I could.

Wednesday, the 27th. I intend to visit a large town of Indians, in order to attempt to preach to them. I intend first to preach to the blacks among them. I am in hopes that if the blacks who can understand English will hear preaching they will influence the Indians to hear me. I go to them not knowing what will be the consequences. I hope it is of the Lord, and that the Lord will open the door for his gospel to be preached to this nation of Indians. Into thy hands, O Lord, I commend myself and the cause in which I am engaged. Thy will be done.

On Thursday, the 28th, I rode about six miles to a town of negroes near a town of Indians called Hickstown. I made my business known to an old man named Pompey, the father and grandfather, and a ruler of them. The old man appeared very glad that I had come to talk to them of the Almighty. They started and let the rest know that I would talk to them. They soon began to gather, making a congregation of about fifty persons.

Sunday, December 14, 1828. To-day I attended the Sabbath school for the last time. The school numbers about twenty. May the Lord bless and preserve the children! At 11 A.M. I preached to a large congregation; at half-past three preached to a large congregation of blacks. At the close four came forward and joined the Church on trial. I preached to a large congregation at night, and at the close of the services many came forward with tears in their eyes to bid me farewell; the colored people also.

On Monday, the 15th, about twelve o'clock, I left Pensacola and rode to Brother Gaines's, about twenty-four miles. I rode next day twenty-seven miles to Brother Briton's, and about midnight started on my journey, and rode fifty-six miles to Claiborne, Ala.

On Thursday I walked to Fort Claiborne. Near the fort is the old burying ground, where lie many soldiers who left their homes and friends to fight for their country, and far from home fell by death's cold hand.

On Friday, 19th, I set out for Tuscaloosa, and, after riding several days, arrived there on the 24th.

On Saturday, the 27th, I visited Bishop Soule, and heard him preach on the next day; also William Winans.

On Monday night four converted Choctaw Indians came into the altar, and by an interpreter they spoke to the audience. A collection of one hundred and seventeen dollars was taken for the Choctaw Mission.

On Thursday, January 1, 1829, I set out for my father's. After riding eight days I arrived at home.

On the 19th I left home for Conference, held at Charleston, S. C.

On Tuesday, the 27th, I arrived at Charleston, and stopped with Mrs. Humphreys, widow of the missionary, who has no doubt gone to receive the faithful missionary's reward.

On Wednesday, 28th, Conference commenced its session; no bishop present except McKendree. On the first day of the Conference I was elected elder.

On Sunday, February 1st, I attended the Cumberland Church, and after a sermon by Dr. Pierce the deacons and elders were ordained by Bishop McKendree.

On September 7th the Conference closed, and appointments were read. I was appointed to the St. Augustine and Alachua Mission. I was much astonished and hurt at the appointment. I hope it will be for the glory of God. I am informed that I am to receive fifty dollars from the missionary society for my support. I have received twelve dollars and fifty cents of the money. I left for my work on the 21st, arrived at St. Augustine on the 23d, and made arrangements to board with Brother Davis.

On Thursday, 24th, visited the old fort to see a man confined for horse stealing. He told me he intended to reform and be a better man. I talked and prayed with him.

On Thursday, 26th, I visited several families, and at night preached in what is called the Government House.

On Sunday, March 1st, I attended the place appointed for worship. Heard Mr. Henderson, an Episcopalian, read a very short sermon. In the evening and at night I preached. I was aided by the good Spirit in both sermons. I trust they were not in vain. On this day, now past forever, I beheld more of the fruits of popery than I ever expected to see. In the afternoon I saw many lads roaming the streets with curious apparel, and bells hung about them ringing, like a stock of cattle. I saw several men, natives of this place, with hands and faces made as black as Ethiopians. They had on very unusual garments and artificial faces; some dressed in women's clothes. Just before sundown I saw about half a dozen females dancing along the streets before a drum and violin some one was playing. The Catholics call such conduct a masquerade.

On Tuesday evening our class met at Brother Davis' house; several whites attended, and about twenty blacks. There was considerable feeling among the blacks, and some among the whites. I feel encouraged that God will revive his work on the mission this year.

On Thursday, 5th of March, I rode thirty-five miles to George Pettrey's, and on the next day preached at St. John's church; met the class after preaching; put up with Mr. Reed for the night.

On Saturday, 7th, rode fifteen miles to Mr. Hendrick's, where I expect to remain until to-morrow. May the Lord pour out his Spirit upon me, and enable me to do his will at all times.

On Sunday, 8th, preached at Jacksonville, and dined with Mrs. Hart, and heard that some members of our church have been dancing. That afternoon I started for Brother Nelson's, got lost, and wandered through the woods in the dark. I got to Brother Nelson's in the night.

On Monday, 9th, rode to Mr. Eubanks', nine miles

from Jacksonville, preached to a small congregation, rode eighteen miles to Brother Phillips'; and the next day left early and rode twenty-five miles to Mr. Johns's, where I preached to a few persons.

On the 13th rode to Dell's Meetinghouse, and found two persons. We prayed together, and I went home with Brother Dell and wife, who were the two persons present.

On Saturday, 14th, rode eighteen miles to Mr. Burnett's, and preached to a few persons.

On Sunday, 15th, I rode six miles and preached. I labored hard; I fear, to no profit.

On Tuesday I rode seventeen miles to Mr. Wanton's and preached. After the meeting closed I made some inquiry about the Indians in Florida. I think the gospel might be preached to them. I feel a great inclination to attempt it.

Wednesday, 18th, I rode forty-five miles to Palatka. Next day I crossed the St. John's river and rode two miles to Brother Rushe's. No one attended preaching.

On Friday, 20th, I rode twenty miles to St. Augustine, and put up at Brother Davis'.

On Sunday, 22d, I preached morning and night, and next day I rode to St. John's meetinghouse and preached.

On the 25th I crossed the river in a small boat. It was so stormy no one attended preaching. I spent the night with Mrs. Hart.

On Sunday, the 5th, I preached in St. Augustine; preached in the evening to the colored people.

On Sunday, the 12th, I preached in Jacksonville.

On Monday, the 13th, I rode to Mr. Gary's, and the next day preached at Black Creek. I wrote a letter to Brother Roberts, living in the Alligator Settlement [now Lake City], stating that if spared I would hold a two-days' meeting in his settlement on the 15th and 16th of August.

On Monday, the 20th, I preached at Wanton's. I had liberty in speaking, but was disturbed by some drunken men.

On Tuesday I rode to the Agency.

On Wednesday, the 22d, I visited Big Swamp and preached to about forty or forty-five blacks. These people heard me gladly. I lectured to them on the relation of the rich man to Lazarus, and showed them the end of the wicked and the righteous. After preaching I was told by some of the most intelligent of the blacks that a great change for the better had taken place with these people since I commenced preaching to them. I afterwards asked another concerning it, and he told me that several of them were leaving off their bad habits. O, may this people continue to reform until they become fearless Christians! After preaching I got an interpreter and set out to visit several chiefs. The first called upon was Olacklimoco. I requested the interpreter to tell him who I was. He said he was glad to see me. I then told him through the interpreter what I had visited him for. He said he had nothing against my preaching to his people, and that he would like to hear me himself, but he could not do anything toward giving me liberty to preach to the Indians until the chiefs assembled together, which would be next Friday. He also stated that he would name my request, and do his best to get the chiefs to grant me the privilege. I am much pleased with the chief, and think that if all the chiefs of the nation were like him it would not be long before the Indians would hear the gospel of Christ. After taking my leave of the chief I, with the interpreter, went to Tuskenah-hah. I conversed with him as I did with Olack-limoco. He observed that I was traveling alone among them. I was certainly trying to do them good. He said he was the governor of that part of the nation, and when the chiefs met at the time already mentioned he would lay my request before them and try and get them to grant it. The interpreter and I then went to John Hicks, who is looked upon by the whites as the chief of the nation. He directly told me he was opposed to the Indians having the gospel preached to them. I labored to convince him that he was in error, but he appeared to regard little what I said. I told him of the Cherokees and Choctaws, who had heard and understood the talk of the Almighty. He observed that they were mixed with the whites and were not full-blooded Indians. I then told him that I had seen several full-blooded Choctaw Indians, and heard two of them speak. He then replied that he had been opposed to preaching, and was determined to continue so. I also told him that persons who would not hear the good word and continued to do bad displeased the Almighty, and when they died would go to the bad world. To this he replied that many of the whites did not attend to the good talk, and that they were as wicked as himself. What a lamentable truth! Will not the heathen rise up at the day of judgment and condemn many who are raised under the sound of the gospel? After finding it useless to speak any more, I parted with the tool of Satan and returned to the Agency about sunset. The influence of Hicks is such that I am afraid he will have a majority of the chiefs in opposing the gospel. If they do oppose, I cannot tell what will be the result; but I am of the opinion that the blacks may be preached to, and if they are I think it will not be long before the prejudices of the Indians will be removed, and then they will gladly hear the gospel. May the Lord hasten the day when the barriers will be removed when these children of the woods shall joyfully hear the gospel, which is able to gladden their hearts during their pilgrimage on earth!

On Thursday, the 23d, I rode to Palatka, a distance of fifty-five miles. Next day 1 crossed the river and preached at Brother Bruskens'.

On Saturday I rode to St. Augustine and put up with Mr. Streeter.

On Sunday, the 26th, I preached in St. Augustine.

CHAPTER V.

Indian Atrocities—John L. Jerry—James B. Jackson— W. M. Crumley—R. H. Howren.

IN 1831 John W. Talley was stationed in Tallahassee, John C. Simmons at St. Augustine and Nassau Mission. Camp meetings were then held in Florida, and were seasons of general revival. This year one was held near Tallahassee. In 1832 our only information is that T. P. C. Shelman was in Tallahassee, and thirty-six members were added to the church. In 1833 J. W. Talley was presiding elder, and James T. Johnson pastor. The district embraced all of Middle Florida, and Decatur, Thomas, and Lowndes Counties in Georgia.

St. Augustine District was served by George A. Chappell, and embraced that part south of the Altamaha.

We can now only give outline of these works; the men who served them have crossed the flood, leaving better places for us who have followed them.

The writer of these imperfect lines often pauses, searches his little library to see if this is all that can be said of these heroic men and their work, but returns to review long stretches of miles—here and there a herdsman's cabin, now and then breaking the forest solitude with songs of praise, here and there gathering a few settlers in a private house and preaching, forming little societies of persons "who earnestly desire to flee from the wrath to come, and to be saved from their sins." But who is the preacher? What are the bounds of his work? From the great white throne it will be answered: "Inasmuch as ye have done it unto one of the least of these my brethren, ye have done it unto me."

During these years J. L. Jerry, James Hutto, John Slade, and others were laboring in East Florida and Southeast Georgia. Dr. Blake has given nearly a full list of presiding elders and pastors of Tallahassee. In 1834 A. H. Mitchell was pastor; in 1835 T. C. Benning was pastor, and Joshua Knowles succeeded him in 1836. During that year he became proprietor of a magazine and remained there some time. He changed his relations later to the Protestant Episcopal Church.

We here insert an extract written by him to Rev. G. G. Smith: "My next appointment was Tallahassee. I arrived there the last Saturday in December, 1835, preached on Sunday, and married my first couple on Sunday night. I was very cordially received by the people. Rev. John L. Jerry was my presiding elder. The Seminole war had just opened, and his district comprised the whole Indian territory. He was a man of courage and zeal, and neither tomahawk nor scalping knife drove him from his work." (Smith, p. 298.) I suppose it will be as well here as elsewhere to give some more extracts from Smith's "History of Methodism in Georgia and Florida:" "In the years 1837 and 1838 in Florida there was call for the highest heroism. The cruel and unconquerable Seminoles were waging exterminating war, and the preachers held their own at the risk of their lives. That grand man, John L. Jerry, whose heart led him to face all dangers, still mustered his band of heroes, and from blockhouse to blockhouse his work moved on. He says in a letter to the *Christian Advocate and Journal:* 'On Monday we heard that the Indians had attacked the house of old Father Baker and killed him, his wife, and one grandchild; the other was found in his arms, though wounded.' He now went to Suwannee with Howren, and preached to a large congregation of officers and citizens, some of whom had come forty miles. 'When I returned home my dear wife was overjoyed to see me. They were expecting an attack on Monticello. She had two pistols, a dirk, and a tomahawk to defend herself and her children.' Yet he and his preachers still went on with their camp meetings. Alas! some of the preachers did not escape so well. Tilman D. Purifoy was returning home when he heard that the Indians had attacked his home and killed his family. He found his wife horribly wounded, but still living. She had been shot by seven balls, tomahawked, and scalped, but strangely recovered. His negroes lay about the yard killed, and his two children, after being murdered, were burned up in the house. This then was the condition of the work in Florida, and these the perils which those brave men had to face." (Page 330.)

"James B. Jackson was admitted on trial in 1838. He had been a very poor boy who worked as a day laborer, and, although quite a youth, could not read. He was employed by a good Presbyterian to pick cotton. The children of the family took great interest in him and taught him his letters. One of the daughters gave him a New Testament, which was then his first and only book. He spelled it through. Its influence and their counsel brought him to Christ. He now applied himself to study, and improved rapidly; he began to teach, was licensed to preach, and entered the Conference. He rose to high place, was on all kinds of work, stations, circuits, and districts, and always did his work well. His mind was very philosophical in cast, he was a fine metaphysician, and perhaps too fond of speculation. After he had been nearly thirty years in active service in Georgia he was transferred to Florida, to meet a demand in that Conference. There was promise of much work before him when, in a railroad accident he was so wounded as to soon die, but not before he had left his testimony to the precious consolations of the truths he had preached." (Page 333.)

"W. M. Crumley was admitted the same year, and appointed to Madison, Fla. Leaving the bleak mountains of Habersham County, Ga., while yet the January snows were on the ground, he made his way over the muddy hills of Middle Georgia, into the wire-grass country. Here he was forced to swim creeks, to travel for almost whole days through the wide sloughs of that flat country. At last he reached his circuit. The people had fled to the blockhouses, and those who were at home were expecting every moment to be forced again to these shelters. He traveled from blockhouse to blockhouse. There was, of course, nothing like Church organization, and the only support accorded to the preacher was that which the people offered without solicitation. He was compelled to travel through long stretches of almost unbroken pine woods to find a home in the cabin of some adventurous stock raiser, or in the hummock country to find shelter with some planter, whom neither exile from society nor dread of Indians could force from his rich cotton fields. To bear all this exposure, and, worse than this, to have a gentle, loving wife to submit to it, was the introduction of this young and timid itinerant to his work. He had left his only child, a little girl, with her grandparents in Habersham, and brought only his young wife with him. The tender parents were very anxious about their child. Crumley had one dollar left when he reached Florida. He found a family almost starving; the husband had been killed by the Indians, and the widow and children were without bread. He gave them his last cent. In Madison he went to the post office, and found a letter from his kinsfolk concerning his daughter, but alas! the postage was twenty-five cents, and he did not have a farthing. Sadly he returned the letter to the postmaster and went to prayer meeting. After it was over the owner of the solitary candle found a five-dollar note in the candlestick. As no one claimed it, he gave it to the preacher. The work on which young Crumley was had to be marked out. The Indians still lurked in the swamps, and often as he traveled his way through the forest he would see where the bullet of an Indian had spilled the blood of a foe. Once he found that the family with whom he had hoped to spend the night had fled to the blockhouse, six miles away, and it was dark. At the great hazard of being shot by the Indians, or mistaken in the dark by the whites as an Indian and shot by them, he reached the fort, and succeeded in making himself known. He passed the year in safety, and was instrumental in the conversion of many souls." (Page 340.)

R. H. Howren was also in Florida, and tells his own story thus:

"It was during the Indian war, when the torch, tomahawk, and rifle were doing their deadly work in this country. My work was mainly with the soldiers, and with citizens clustered together under stockade protection. I knew that I was exposed to sudden and violent death every day, but the divine promise sustained me: 'Lo, I am with you alway, even unto the end of the world.'

"On one occasion, while holding a protracted meeting near Newnansville, we were surrounded by seventy-five warriors, who withdrew without interfering with us at all. We learned afterwards that their intention was to make an attack upon us, but seeing such an unusual stir among the people, they became alarmed and withdrew. During one of our night services, they climbed into the pines around the house, intending to fire upon us, not being able to do so from the ground owing to the stockade. Fortunately we heard the signal given for firing, and ran into the body of the house and escaped. One of our local preachers, Brother McCrary, was shot from his horse and killed while returning from one of his appointments Sabbath afternoon. He was in company with a Mr. McNeil, who escaped with four balls through his clothes and two in his horse. The noble animal, though badly wounded, sprang forward and soon bore his rider beyond the reach of danger. A little boy, twelve years of age, riding a little behind, wheeled his pony and took the other end of the road, a large Indian jumping into the road nearly opposite the boy. The race was nearly equal for a hundred yards or more, the savage making several reaches for the bridle, but at length the lad outstripped him and escaped in safety to the fort. Brother McCrary was talking to his unconverted friend on the subject of religion when the guns were fired. How literally he realized the poet's hope:

> Happy, if with my latest breath
> I may but gasp his name;
> Preach him to all, and cry in death,
> "Behold, behold the Lamb!"

The war continued until 1842, when a treaty was made and hostilities ceased; there was still danger, and an occasional massacre. The last one was that of Mrs. Crum. She, her daughter, Mrs. Harn, her granddaughter, Miss Mary Harn, and Mr. J. F. MacDonell were riding, the latter driving the carriage, and Mrs. Harn riding on horseback. A number of Indians fired upon them. Mr. MacDonell was shot through the chest, but sprang into the bushes and escaped. Mrs. Crum was killed. Mrs. Harn caught her daughter by the arm, assisted her upon the horse, and they escaped. I have heard this related by each of the survivors. Mr. MacDonell lived to an old age, raised a large family, was honored and loved in his county, and passed to his reward in January, 1894.

The seven years' war was now ended. Many of the former citizens of Florida returned. From many States new settlers came to build up homes and fortunes in the Land of Flowers, and with them came many heralds of the cross whose objects were the cultivation of "Immanuel's land," so that in 1843 and 1844 the territory was largely occupied, missions extending from Tampa Bay and Indian River to the Georgia line, from the Atlantic to the Apalachicola River. Districts were laid out, and stations, circuits, and missions organized, and the field largely prepared for the organization of the Florida Conference.

PART III.

CHAPTER I.

The Author Transferred to the Florida Conference.

WE now come to the part of this work in which the writer was a participant, and before proceeding I will state that I was born in Burke County, Ga., December 20, 1822; was converted August 25, 1837; was licensed to exhort December 22, 1842; and received my license to preach December 16, 1843. The health of my uncle, the Rev. J. B. Chappell, failing on his way from Conference in January, 1844, I was placed on the Carnesville Circuit in his place, which I served to the close of the year. I was admitted into the Georgia Conference at Eatonton in January, 1845, and with seven others was transferred to the Florida Conference, taking my place in the class of the first year; was ordained deacon by Bishop Capers two years afterwards, and elder by the same bishop two years from that time. I am aware that the object of our Conference in asking me to write these reminiscences was to preserve from oblivion the names of persons and incidents which should not be lost, but in assuming the task I realize the danger of apparent egotism or dull monotony. The mere stringing together of names and incidents would gain but few readers; the elaboration of these would swell the volume quite beyond the design of the author. We propose to take the subject chronologically, giving in the main an outline of our Conferences, with the names of the men who composed them, a general glance at the work, with such incidents as have come under my observation, or are well authenticated, as I may think will interest the reader.

CHAPTER II.

Our First Conference and Its Members.

The first Florida Conference convened in Tallahassee February 6, 1845, Bishop Soule presiding, and Thomas C. Benning, Secretary. It embraced all Middle and East Florida, and that part of Georgia lying south of Fort Gaines, Albany, and the Altamaha River.

There were (including transfers) twelve elders—namely, John Slade, Thomas C. Benning, P. P. Smith, J. W. Yarbrough, T. W. Cooper, R. H. Howren, A. Martin, A. Peeler, W. W. Griffin, S. P. Richardson, A. J. Deavours, and J. J. Richards. Of the class of the third year: J. W. Mills, A. D. Russell. Of the second year: James Harris, G. A. Mallette, N. R. Fleming, J. N. Miner, E. L. T. Blake, and John Penny. Of the first year: S. G. Chiles, D. L. White, F. A. Johnson, and A. Graham. Of those admitted: R. A. Griffin, G. C. Clarke, G. W. Pratt, J. M. N. Low, J. Carraway, J. H. Bryan, and John C. Ley.

Thirty-one in all constituted the forlorn hope to lead the hosts of God's elect from Key West to Albany, from the Atlantic to Apalachicola. No wonder our venerable bishop exclaimed on reading our appointments: "When I look over your vast territory and the needs of your work, I almost wish myself a young man and a member of the Florida Conference." But by making circuits extend over as much territory as is now covered by districts, and the preachers serving seven appointments in the week, and with supplies from the local ranks, the work was manned. Four districts were formed and served by R. H. Luckey, P. P. Smith, T. C. Benning, and J. W. Yarbrough.

On the 11th of February we received appointments, and with the blessing of our bishop bade farewell to each other, turned our faces toward our fields of labor, with our parting hymn ringing in our ears:

> The vineyard of the Lord
> Before his lab'rers lies;
> And lo! we see the vast reward
> Which waits us in the skies.

In tracing the brief journal kept by me at that time memory places me again in that Conference. I love to linger among the heroes of that little band, now nearly all passed away. But one answers to roll call now in our Conference, and as far as I know only S. P. Richardson, in the North Georgia Conference, and the author of these lines survive. But the men of that day rise before me, the men, the work, yea, the very spirit that animated them. Here is R. A. Griffin, a young man of about thirty years of age just entering the work. He goes to Chucochattee, next to Newnansville, thence to Hamilton, where, in 1846, he ends his labors in holy triumph, leaving to his brethren an untarnished name and a worthy example.

Here is a man of middle age, prematurely gray; small, straight, nervous, a piercing eye, impulsive. He would be marked in any deliberative body. He goes to Madison, thence to St. Mary's District, and is sent as delegate to the General Conference in 1846,

This year he breaks down. Consumption has its fangs upon him; he settles in Tampa, laboring to build up our little church. In 1850, in the presence of the author and two other ministers, he takes the sacrament, and talks of death as calmly as if it were only an ordinary journey. In the midst of friends, engaged in conversation, a slight tremor, and the spirit of Alexander Martin has passed to his reward, the second from our little band.

The author was sent this year to Ocean Pond Mission. It embraced all of what is now Bradford, part of Columbia, Hamilton, and Suwannee Counties, Florida, and part of Camden, Ga. The extremes were Fort Call, Yelvington's, and Sweat's in "the big bend" (Georgia), Blount's Ferry, southwest of the Okefinokee Swamp, through Hamilton County, via Echeetucknee and Fort White to Fort Call. There was no post office, church, or school house in the mission. I received my mail at Newnansville each round. The seven years' war had recently closed, and settlers had rushed to this region for the range. They had formed into settlements or colonies, sometimes twenty or thirty miles apart, for mutual protection. I traveled on horseback by pocket compass, often receiving such directions as this: "Keep this course [pointing] for ten miles, and you will strike an Indian trail, take the left-hand end, and it will carry you in about five miles of the settlement."

The country was generally open, no obstructions except an occasional pond to be surrounded, or a branch or cypress slough to be forded. But in the rainy season the Suwannee, Santa Fé, New River, Cypress Creek, and three prongs of St. Mary's River were all often swimming; but by this time the missionary had learned the routes, and had become a fair woodsman. The weather was warm, and it required no great heroism to shoulder saddlebags and umbrella and take a pleasant bath while his faithful horse bore him in safety to the other shore. I have often looked with pity upon the poor specimen of humanity, whom God has honored by "putting him into the ministry," when I have heard him croak and complain of its hardships and sacrifices.

The appointments on this work were first filled in two weeks, but as their number increased, they covered three. So the preacher was in the saddle or preaching, or both, seven days in each week.

There were no church buildings in the mission. The settlers opened their doors, and their neighbors came together; but the latter part of this year we built at Fort Call a church of pine poles, and hewed puncheons for floor and seats. We sawed out doors and windows, made a rude table, and the building was complete. It would doubtless have compared poorly with St. Peter's, yet we can say with triumph of our Zion: "This and that man was born there." As I pen these lines, the names of Benjamin Moody, William Futch, Mrs. Yelvington, Messrs. Blackwelder, King, and a host of others who were friends of the Church, and of the "boy preacher" of those days, rise before me. God bless their sons and daughters! Their fathers and mothers have "fallen on sleep."

CHAPTER III.

Second Conference—The Armed Occupation Act—A. J. Deavours—Extracts from Journal.

OUR Conference held its second session in Monticello February 9, 1846, Bishop Andrew, President; P. P. Smith, Secretary. George J. Arnow, Franklin Stewart, Thomas Taylor, and J. W. Carlton were admitted. John L. Jerry, J. J. Taylor, and M. Bedell were readmitted. T. C. Benning, Anderson Peeler, J. N. Miner, and N. R. Fleming were located. Of these, Thomas C. Benning was afterwards admitted into the Protestant Methodist Church, and died in Brooklyn, N. Y., a few years since. J. N. Miner remained a local preacher in Florida a few years. He left under a cloud. His end I know not. N. R. Fleming read medicine and was practicing in Lincoln County, Ga., the last I knew of him. A. Peeler engaged in the practice of medicine and served the Church as a local preacher until 1872, when he was readmitted. He served the Church faithfully until called to his reward.

In manning the work this year the only change in the districts was A. Martin vice T. C. Benning, on the St. Mary's. The writer was sent to Benton Mission.

For the purpose of settling out the Indians, Congress had passed what is known as the "armed occupation act." It provided that any man who would settle south of a given line, keep a gun and so much ammunition, build a house fit for the habitation of man, cultivate five acres of land, and remain on it five years, should receive a patent for one hundred and sixty acres of land. As there were then but few massacres reported, the lands being fine, there was a rush for the prize, especially as this was the only hope of many of the settlers ever owning land. They were mostly unmarried men, and those who had families generally left them in places of greater safety. Among the early immigrants A. J. Deavours is found preaching and singing in their forest homes.

> No more shall the sound of the war whoop be heard,
> The ambush and slaughter no longer be feared,
> The tomahawk, buried, shall rest in the ground,
> And peace and good will to the nations abound.

I love to think of that noble pioneer missionary. Full of love, full of zeal, no danger daunts him, no hardships discourage him. The love of souls was the all-consuming fire that burned in his bones. He served mission fields a few years, then returned to Georgia.

When the author reached his mission it was to find the general discouragement which follows an enthusiasm that never pauses to count the cost. The houses "fit for the habitation of man" had been generally built by driving four forked poles into the ground, for plates, rafters, etc., the same kind of poles, these fastened with withes or vines; thatching the sides and roofs with the broad palmetto leaves, the house was completed and "fit for the habitation of man." The farm was equally elaborate. The furniture and fare were in keeping with the surroundings. Here the missionary ate and prayed with the family (only one man), slept with his host, and the next day preached to him and his neighbors.

The little money the emigrant carried with him had generally been spent, and now the question was: "After suffering so much, shall I abandon all and go back to my friends, or shall I try to weather it through and save my land?" The preacher who traveled this work had some of what the world calls hardships, but we did not feel them very hard. "There is a silver lining to every cloud," and our trials were mingled with joys. We adopted as our motto: "Wherever men can go for money, we can go for the love of Christ and for souls."

A few extracts from our journal may interest the reader:

May 4.—This morning I left Brother Harn's, Benton County, Fla., in company with J. W. Yarbrough, presiding elder, to attend the first quarterly meeting ever held in Orange County. We made arrangements for crossing the head waters of the Withlacoochee, they being swollen. Two men accompanied us to the first and main branch. Running our vehicles one at a time over a canoe until the axle rested upon the gunwales, two men swam beside and pushed to the other shore. Getting all across, we harnessed up and resumed our journey, the men returning home. On reaching the second branch we found an old broken military bridge sunk down in the middle. Cutting poles and throwing them across the chasm, we *slid* our carriages safely to the other shore, swimming our horses across; then we harnessed up and proceeded. A short drive brought us to the place of "Dade's Massacre." Here we paused and inspected the field. The trees scarred by bullets, the logs used for improvised breastworks, the open graves from which the bodies of that noble band had recently been taken and carried to St. Augustine for interment, made impressions upon my mind I can never describe. About 9 P.M. we reached a house, having narrowly escaped being upset in a bad ford after dark. We gave thanks to God for protection, and retired to rest.

May 5.—This morning we resumed our journey, but during the forenoon our trail utterly gave out. Retracing our steps some miles, we struck the right trail. About 3 P.M., in coming out of a bad ford, my horse broke one of my sulky's wheels. Brother Yarbrough took my trunk, and a walk of about five miles brought us to the home of Brother E. J. Harris, the first house we had seen since morning.

May 6.—Borrowing a saddle, we resumed our journey, and about 4 P.M. reached the house of Mrs. Rogers (where Apopka City now stands), the only house or person we had seen during the day.

May 7.—This afternoon we reached Fort Melon, having seen no man or human habitation during the day. We were the guests of Dr. Speer, and comforts and luxuries we relished. Our quarterly meeting was one of interest. John Penny was the missionary.

May 11.—This morning, having enjoyed the hospitality of friends and the presence of the Lord in our meeting, we started back, reaching Mrs. Rogers' just before night.

May 12.—Resumed our journey, but before night my horse gave out, and we stopped in the road. He had been a stranger to sufficient food for a long time, but by resting him and walking I reached Brother Harris' a little after dark.

May 13.—This morning I took an ax and walked out to the place where I had left my sulky, cut a pole and lashed it to the shaft under the axle, piled up the *débris*, and led my horse back to Brother Harris', and rested until morning. Then came "the tug of war." It was seventy-five miles to the nearest shop; so availing myself of a few farm tools, I sawed some dry white oak rails and made spokes, drove them into the hub, placed the fellies as near as possible equidistant from the center, cut tenons, drove them on, then heated the tire, and with the assistance of the family, tongs, and poker, we soon had a wheel, not quite as neat as I have seen, but it answered my purpose.

May 14.—Started to-day for my work, and before night my horse again gave out, but by resting, coaxing, and walking I reached a house before night. Here I succeeded in buying a pony by giving my horse in the trade.

July 26.—To-day I preached at Tampa, opened the doors of the Church, and organized a society, the first ever organized in this place. Dr. J. Roberts was appointed class leader. O that the little vine may continue to spread and fill all these lands!

This was a year of general prosperity in our Conference; though the minutes only show an increase of one hundred and seventy-two whites, and two hundree and twenty-five colored members, still the work was gaining in form and strength.

CHAPTER IV.

Our Third Conference—Hamilton Circuit—Affliction.

OUR third Conference convened in Quincy, Bishop Capers presiding. Moses C. Smith, Samuel Woodbury, Nelson Conner, I. N. Craven, John McPhail, and Leroy G. Leslie were admitted. Ira L. Potter, Henry T. Jones, and Joseph J. Sealey were received by transfer; J. W. Yarbrough, F. A. Johnson, and J. H. Bryan located; G. J. Arnow and J. W. Carlton were discontinued; R. A. Griffin had been removed by death, and A. J. Deavours by transfer, leaving a net increase of only two men. Of those leaving us, J. W. Yarbrough was a strong and earnest preacher. To Georgia his history belongs. F. A. Johnson was a young man of good mind but limited education. He served the Church many years as a local preacher. J. H. Bryan went to his plantation. J. W. Carlton was a man of feeble health and fervent piety. G. J. Arnow went into the practice of law, and now resides in Gainesville.

This year J. L. Jerry was sent to the Newnansville District, and James Harris to the St. Mary's. I was sent to Hamilton Circuit. On my way to my work, being very weak from protracted fevers the previous year, I was attacked with pneumonia in Monticello, where I remained for several days, and then started, very feeble, and my mouth very sore from salivation. On reaching my work I found the streams all swollen, which required frequent swimming. One day I swam three streams, while heavy rains fell much of the time. On reaching a house near night, my clothes all wet and no chance for drying, my mouth still very sore, and not enough covering to keep me warm had I been dry, I passed an uncomfortable night. Yet the God that takes note of the sparrows shielded me, so that I experienced no bad effects from this temporary discomfort. The year was one of general prosperity on the circuit, accessions at all the appointments. Our camp meeting at Swift Creek October 25 was a time of general refreshing and great power. There were many conversions, and nineteen accessions to the church. The following is an extract from my journal:

"*December 25.*—To-day I meet my dear mother and sister after an absence of two years. Glory be to God for all his mercies! In the darkest hours through which I have passed since I was last here he has sustained me. My body has been afflicted, yet my soul has triumphed. When all hope of life was gone I could say: 'The will of the Lord be done.' He has raised me up and enabled me to again meet my loved ones, and now I vow to endeavor to be more faithful and humble. May the grace of God ever sustain me! for I am sure that unsaved by him I fall."

Our fourth Conference convened in Waynesville, Ga., February 9, 1848, Bishop Andrew presiding, and P. P. Smith Secretary. Wm. M. Kennedy and Robert S. Tucker were admitted; G. W. Fagg was received by transfer; H. T. Jones and David L. White located; I. N. Craven and John McPhail discontinued; T. W. Cooper and J. M. N. Low were permitted to rest on account of feeble health, leaving a decrease of four from the effective list. Of those leaving our ranks, D. L. White was a son of Dr. D. L. White, of Quincy. He was a young man of liberal education, deep piety, and sterling worth. He settled at Iola, where for many years he did good service as a local preacher, until some years ago he passed to his reward, leaving a widow, a son, and three daughters. The daughters have since then, all in triumph, crossed the flood. The widow and son still live, and labor for and contribute liberally to the Church. J. J. Taylor returned to his plantation in Columbia County, where he rendered good service to the Church until called to his reward. The writer was sent this year to St. Mary's Station. The charge was small, the situation pleasant. Among the many friends of that year I must mention the families of Mrs. Seals and Mr. A. J. Bessent, in whose houses I found homes, and whose kindness and hospitality have ever been cherished among the reminiscences of my early ministry.

CHAPTER V.

From 1849 to 1853.

OUR fifth session met in Albany, Ga., January 31, 1849, Bishop Capers, President; P. P. Smith, Secretary. O. B. Stanley, J. M. Hendry, J. H. M. Gardner, and T. N. Gardner were admitted. W. M. Choice was readmitted. Mr. Choice was born in Hancock County, Ga., in January, 1800; was admitted into the Georgia Conference in 1832; served the Leon Circuit in 1833 and 1834, the St. Mary's District from 1837 to 1839, Jacksonville District in 1840 and 1841; located and was supply on the Tallahassee Station in 1842 and 1843. During this period there was a wonderful revival, and many of our members there to-day are either converts or children of converts of that revival. From his readmission until his death he was a useful and faithful preacher. He was a stout man, with florid complexion, and a powerful voice. It is said that in preaching his farewell sermon in St. Mary's he exclaimed, "You may never hear my *feeble* voice again," though that voice was heard two miles. He was earnest and had many seals to his ministry. Passing from us in 1855, he said: "I am going to die, but I am ready."

This year I was sent to Albany Station, and on the 1st of May was married to Miss Ann Eliza Wade. She was stepdaughter of Dr. White, of Quincy. She was about my age, educated, refined, pious, and lovely—in all respects adapted to the life of the helpmeet of an itinerant preacher.

During this year we had a revival of considerable power, which was renewed the following year under the ministry of Mr. Brady, which gave much strength to our church in that city.

Our sixth Conference held its session in Madison. In the absence of Bishop Andrew, Ira L. Potter was elected President, and P. P. Smith, Secretary. Aaron W. Harris, William C. Brady, John W. Carlton, and James K. Conner were admitted. Anderson Peeler was readmitted. James Peeler, J. P. Richardson, J. M. Valentine, and Philip Pelly were received by transfer. John W. Mills, George W. Fagg, Moses C. Smith, and Augustus D. Russell located. Three were allowed to rest on account of feeble health.

This year I was sent to Marion Circuit, which extended from Pilatlacaha on the south to St. Augustine on the northeast. During the year we gave an appointment to Palatka, preaching in the courthouse. I think there were no houses there then, except such as had been erected during the war for military purposes. There were two stores, kept by R. R. Reed and K. R. Duke. I should think there were from twelve to twenty families. We organized a society of about fifteen members, which still exists. True, the members that then constituted the roll have passed to the other shore, but others have taken their places. As the place changed from a village to a city, others came in, and with help from abroad built churches, but our little band was unable to build. About 1860, through the efforts of the members and the energy of Revs. William Davies and William E. Collier, a plain house was erected. It stood as a place for worship for many years, but, small and unsightly, it was more a type of weakness than of strength. While writing about this place I will state that in 1884 Palatka was made a station and J. B. Ley was sent to it, where he remained four years, during which time they built a parsonage and a pretty and commodious church.

The most important point on the circuit was Ocala. In 1846 the county seat of Marion was moved here. At the time I came to the circuit, there was a courthouse built of pine poles, which served for all public purposes. It served as a church for all denominations, also as a public hall and theater.

There were three stores kept by Messrs. Tison & Harris, E. D. House, and A. Waterman, a doggery and post office south of the square kept by William Roberts, and a small hotel where the Ocala House now stands. I suppose some twelve or fifteen families constituted the town. The missionary had been here and a society had been organized.

This year we secured the lots for our church, but were unable to do anything more toward a house of worship.

On the 5th of March of this year God called my young and loving wife from earth to her reward. Only about eleven months was she lent to me; then she was translated to a fairer clime. In attempting to account for this dispensation of God's providence I was almost wrecked, but the same loving Father which has always sustained me enabled me finally to realize that he is good, and that "all things work together for good to them that love God." "What I do thou knowest not now; but thou shalt know hereafter."

The year as a whole was one of prosperity in our Conference, giving us a net increase of one thousand and ninety-five whites, and five hundred and ninety-two colored members. Two of our preachers had died, Alexander Martin and James R. Conner. Mr. Conner was a young man of deep piety, an earnest and useful man; but in the morning of life, with prospects of usefulness before him, God called him from labor to rest.

The seventh session of our Conference convened in Thomasville, Ga., January 9, 1851; Bishop Paine presiding, and P. P. Smith, Secretary.

William Edwards and David R. Kellog were admitted, F. A. Johnson was readmitted, R. M. Tydings received by transfer, G. A. Mallette and L. G. Lesley located, P. Pelly and N. Conner removed by transfer.

The stewards settled with claimants at sixty-five cents on the dollar, the best we had ever done.

The writer was sent to Palatka and St. Augustine Mission, but the health of J. M. Valentine failing soon after Conference, I was changed to the Jacksonville Station, which I served the remainder of that year.

Our eighth session met in Tallahassee January 28, 1852. In the absence of Bishop Andrew, W. W. Griffin was elected President, and P. P. Smith, Secretary.

Samuel A. McCook, Peter B. Bedford, and William H. Turner were admitted; J. W. Mills and G. W. Fagg were readmitted; Thomas Gardner was received from the Protestant Methodist Church; J. M. N. Low and T. W. Cooper took no appointment on account of feeble health; George C. Clarke was transferred to Georgia, and Alexander Graham was sent as missionary to California—leaving a net increase of six to our itinerant ranks. S. P. Richardson was sent to the Tallahassee District, and Franklin Stewart to the St. Mary's District. I was returned to Jacksonville.

This year was one of general prosperity in our Conference. In Jacksonville we nearly doubled our membership, repaired and painted our church, and more than doubled our congregation. The Tallahassee District was blessed with general revival power and large increase of members. Our net increase was four hundred and fifty-one whites, and three hundred and eighty-nine blacks.

Our financial showing was not an enviable one, as we settled with claimants at thirty-eight and one-half cents on the dollar. When we remember that one hundred dollars was the maximum of a single preacher's salary, there was not much need of urging upon us the caution: "If riches increase, set not your heart upon them."

The Conference held its ninth session in Quincy, beginning January 26, 1853, Bishop Capers in the chair.

F. R. C. Ellis and John F. Rivers were admitted.

The districts were served by S. P. Richardson, R. H. Howren, F. Stewart, and G. W. Pratt.

The writer was sent to St. Mary's Station. Here we found the church almost broken up by divisions growing out of troubles of the previous year. But while unable to heal many of the wounds, we were successful in some respects, and passed the year pleasantly with some degree of success.

On the 4th of July of this year I was married to Miss Martha S. Pottle. For over forty-four years she has been the partner of my joys and sorrows, my hopes and fears. Both in prosperity and adversity, in sickness and in health, we have walked the path of life together. God gave us three sons, all of whom still live and have families of their own. Two of them are members of our Conference, and the other is a devout Christian and a zealous worker in the Church. My wife still lives (1897), to aid and comfort me in my itinerant work.

CHAPTER VI.

From 1854 to 1858.

OUR tenth Conference convened in Monticello. R. H. Howren was elected President, and P. P. Smith, Secretary. James W. Jackson, Archibald Johnson, Robert I. McCooke, and William Peeler were admitted.

At this Conference the Thomasville District was formed. I was returned to St. Mary's, and this year had my first experience with yellow fever. It proved a terrible scourge, some whole families passing away, and scarcely any that were not decimated. It was estimated that one-fifth of the white people who remained in town died. I was the fourth person taken down, having officiated at the funerals of the previous three. Although my attack was a very violent one, yet through the skill of my physician, good nursing, and, above all, the kind hand of my Heavenly Father, I was able to walk about a little in ten days. From this time I was engaged night and day, praying for and administering to the sick, counseling with the families, and burying the dead. The epidemic lasted about three months, and for several weeks I attended more or less funerals every day. At about the height of the scourge my wife was taken. In almost every house there was sickness. Nurses were scarce, for we had no professionals at that time. Doctors were overworked, and were absolutely unable to meet the actual needs of the suffering. For nine days I did not undress, the little sleep I got being in snatches of a few moments at a time. One night I can never forget. It was about the crisis of my wife's illness. I was watching alone, when just in front of my door there was a scream of a female's voice; such a voice as I never heard equaled in power and clearness. The shriek was followed by a torrent of blasphemy and vulgarity, which I think I have never heard equaled. The darkness of the night, the hour (about 12 P.M.), the distress in the town, my own heart bleeding for the one I was watching, with the fearful cursing outside, produced a feeling language fails to describe. It was a poor crazy woman, a wanderer, who had come into town a few days before.

The epidemic finally passed away, leaving many sad memories, none of which were more sad than the fact that the people failed to learn righteousness. The devotees of pleasure and dissipation seemed to vie with each other to regain what they had lost by the scourge.

The eleventh session of our Conference met in December, 1854, in Madison. This was the last Conference over which the sainted Bishop Capers presided. Going home from this, he was attacked with heart disease in a few days, and soon passed to his reward.

We admitted on trial David L. Kennedy, Martin V. Wells, James T. Stockton, James O. Branch, Francis A. Branch, John L. Williams, Francis M. Wilson, and Amos Davis.

The writer was sent to Thomasville Station. Owing to family affairs, my own health, and some circumstances connected with the making of this appointment, it was the most afflictive that I had ever received. But God overruled all for good, and it proved one of the pleasantest charges I ever served. Here God gave us our first son. And here let me record that through life the rule has been that appointments received with the greatest pleasure have often had their greatest trials, and those which have been received with the saddest feelings have proved among the most successful and pleasant.

Our twelfth Conference was held in Bainbridge, Ga., December, 1855. In the absence of Bishop Andrew, S. P. Richardson was elected President, serving until the arrival of the bishop. The country at the time was flooded with rain, water courses swimming. The first day less than half the preachers were present. The following day many others arrived, and by the close of Conference nearly all were present, having overcome many difficulties and dangers.

We admitted on trial Joseph A. W. Johns, Valerius C. Cannon, Grandison Royster, Thomas R. Barnett, Samuel S. Cobb, Willis P. Ocain, Thomas A. Carruth, John F. Andrews, Theophilus J. Johnson, Charles P. Murdock, Robert F. Lanier, James M. Points, Isaac A. Towers, and James A. McCollum, a much larger class than at any previous Conference.

The increase of members was one thousand six hundred and seventy-three. The work was largely rearranged and divided into seven districts, which were served by J. R. Plummer, William M. Kennedy, P. P. Smith, J. W. Mills, T. N. Gardner, J. C. Ley, and G. W. Pratt.

I went to Jacksonville and R. M. Tydings went to the station. We found the church in Jacksonville in a desperate condition. There had been an extensive revival the previous year under the ministry of D. B.

Lynne, but after the revival there were varied troubles, and the pastor, though a great revivalist, was not a success in managing Church difficulties.

We commenced a series of protracted services soon after Conference, which continued through several weeks. Some were converted, many reclaimed, many deep wounds were healed; but alas! some were too deep, and the parties left the Church. Yet in that charge it was a year of prosperity. My district extended from the Georgia line, embracing Orange County, from the Atlantic to the Gulf, yet in the whole district we had but three ordained pastors. In most places the children and adult members could not receive baptism, and some who had been members for years had never had the privilege of taking the sacrament of the Lord's Supper. To meet these necessities, I arranged with the preachers to hold services at different places each week between quarterly meeting, and administer the ordinances. But the work I soon found was beyond my strength, and taking measles, which settled in my bowels, I was able to do but little work the last part of the year.

At that time we had at Micanopy a Conference seminary. We had, as we thought, made good arrangements for instructors for the fall, but a few weeks before the time for opening we received notice of disappointment in our plans. It was too late to procure teachers, and it was thought another disappointment would cause the entire enterprise to prove a failure.

The state of my health, the necessities of the seminary, with the earnest entreaties of the trustees and such of the preachers of the district as could be consulted, induced me to make the best arrangements I could for my last round and accept the position of Principal of the seminary, Mrs. Ley taking charge of the female department.

I will here state what I have to say in regard to this enterprise. It was started about 1857 under the management of Rev. J. M. Hendry, Agent. A substantial house had been erected, and school opened, but some debts upon the building, and these increased by deficiency on teachers' salaries, had accumulated until there seemed but little hope of saving the property. The whole would not have sold for enough to liquidate the debts. The Conference for 1856 had appointed a new Board of Trustees. We obtained time and had nearly liquidated the debts, with a respectable nucleus for endowment, and a patronage of over one hundred students; but discord among patrons caused me to resign at the close of 1859. The local troubles, and the war, which called off most of the young men, caused the seminary to be closed in the latter part of 1860. After the war the fearful state of finances forced it to be sold for a trifle, and thus it passed from our hands.

Our thirteenth session was held at Alligator (now Lake City), Bishop Andrew presiding, and P. P. Smith, Secretary. We admitted B. J. Johnson, J. J. Giles, Leroy B. Giles, J. E. Darden, W. G. M. Quarterman, and J. K. Glover. T. W. Cooper was readmitted. J. M. Davis, E. F. Gates, J. M. Wright, and J. W. Timberlake were received by transfer. Edward G. Asey was expelled.

Our fourteenth session was held in Thomasville, Bishop Early presiding, and P. P. Smith, Secretary. H. G. Townsend, William Williams, Henry F. Smith,

William A. Dyall, Isaac Mundan, Robert A. Carson, O. A. Myers, and J. Rast were admitted.

Our Conference held its fifteenth session in Jacksonville, Bishop Andrew presiding, and J. C. Ley, Secretary, beginning December 15, 1858. E. H. Giles, J. Henderson, J. Stewart, J. A. Hemingway, P. A. McCook, F. B. Davis, S. R. Weaver, J. P. Holmes, W. C. Jourdan, and R. L. Wiggins were admitted.

The past year had been one of general prosperity and one thousand eight hundred and fourteen members had been added to the church. Extensive revivals were reported in nearly all parts of the Conference.

CHAPTER VII.

From 1860 to 1863.

The sixteenth session of our Conference was held in Micanopy, beginning December 28, 1859, Bishop Kavanaugh presiding, and P. P. Smith, Secretary.

Robert E. Evans, William F. Roberts, Robert W. Flournoy, Andrew R. Bird, Cornelius Parker, James D. Maulding, James L. Carruth, R. R. Burts, Sterling Gardner, J. M. Bridges, and David D. Henry were admitted on trial. Joseph J. Sealey, J. W. Jackson, and Robert W. Burges were readmitted. John R. Harwell was received by transfer. Joshua Carraway, J. Anderson, and Willis P. Ocain were supernumerary. E. L. T. Blake, John Penny, M. Bedell, William Edwards, Thomas Taylor, and Jesse M. Valentine were superannuated. O. B. Stanley was removed by transfer. John L. Jerry has passed to his reward, leaving a net increase to our effective force of fifteen.

We still had six districts, served by S. P. Richardson, S. Woodbury, David L. Kennedy, T. W. Cooper, J. W. Mills, and W. L. Murphy.

Soon after Conference Micanopy was scourged with a severe visitation of pneumonia. Many persons died, among them Revs. T. W. Cooper and William Edwards. Bishop Kavanaugh removed me from Flemington Mission to the St. John's District, to fill the vacancy occasioned by the death of Brother Cooper. The work extended from the St. Mary's River to Indian River, and had to be served mostly by private conveyance. The traveler of to-day can form but little conception of what it was then. The country was but thinly settled, often there were stretches of forty miles between houses. The roads, especially in the southern part of the district, were chiefly such as had been opened by the troops during the Indian war. The rapid growth of vegetation rendered the roads obscure, and often, for miles, the traveler did not know whether he was on the right road or not; indeed, he was often perplexed to find out if he was on any road. But in all such cases of uncertainty he well knew that the country was broad, and there was plenty of room in the woods in which to lodge. And if he could keep out of too deep water, he would get somewhere sometime, and that wherever he reached a human habitation a cordial welcome awaited him, and that when he reached the place for preaching he would meet an eager congregation, some of whom had come many miles to hear the word. I sometimes meet some to whom I preached in those days, and as old soldiers we joyfully rehearse the battles fought, but most of them have crossed the flood.

There were also many things to amuse the weary pilgrim, and by way of contrast between then and now I shall introduce the substance of a dialogue between the writer and a young man who had come over twenty miles to the meeting:

"Can't you send us a passun to preach at F. next year?"

"What is the distance from your settlement to the nearest place of preaching?"

"Over twenty miles."

"How many families live in your settlement?"

"About twenty."

"Has no minister ever visited and preached to them."

"I have hearn that a passun came down once, but he never come back. I suppose they did not take keer uv him, for you know it is the natur uv um to go where they are taken good keer uv."

In that county we then had one young (single) missionary; we now (1897) have seven regular pastoral charges and as many ministers.

The character of travel on this work often caused my absence from home from four to six weeks, for while the distance was too great to go and return each week, it was comparatively light to go from one quarterly meeting to the next. In these long trips my wife sometimes accompanied me, and while on one of these trips in Orange County she fell from an unfinished house, where we lodged, and came near losing her life. This compelled my returning home as soon as she could be carried, and also necessitated my asking the bishop to release me from the district at our next Conference.

The year had been one of prosperity to our Conference, giving an increase of two hundred and forty-eight whites and two hundred and ninety-two colored members.

This fall Abraham Lincoln was elected President; and here began our fearful struggle, the four years of the civil war. It is not my design to trace the scenes of that fraternal strife, much less to enter into the great questions of causes and effects underlying the acts which brought about the war. We propose to allude to the war only as it affected the operations of the Church.

The year 1860 took from us by death Thomas W. Cooper, one of our finest declaimers. In pathos he had few equals. His health had always been feeble, hence his zeal was far beyond his strength. From the year 1840 he had been in Florida, and wherever he went revivals attended his ministry. But in a short time his health would fail, requiring a year's rest or a location. But upon improving health he would return to the regular work. After some years' rest he had been readmitted and served the Tampa District four years. At our last Conference he was transferred to the St. John's District, beginning his work with zeal. The Sunday before his death he preached with power in Micanopy, where he lived. On Tuesday he was taken with putrid sore throat, and strong pneumonic symptoms, and in a few days passed away in triumph, February 24, 1860.

William Edwards also died this year. He was a lovely man. Though not brilliant, he was earnest and faithful, and for ten years had rendered efficient service in the Conference. He also died in Micanopy March 15, 1860. His end was peace. While I stood by his dying bed his faith gave me a fresh inspiration of the power of grace to draw the last sting of death.

Our Conference held its seventeenth session in Monticello, commencing December 12, 1860, Bishop Pierce presiding, and P. P. Smith, Secretary.

W. F. Easterling, Jephthah Lee, J. F. Urquhart, Josiah Bullock, J. J. Snow, and G. R. Frisbee were admitted on trial; J. M. Hendry was readmitted; H. T. Lewis, S. E. Randolph, and A. J. Wooldrich were received by transfer; J. J. Sealey, G. Royster, T. N.

Gardner, and P. H. McCook located. Two were removed by death and one by transfer, leaving a net gain to our ministerial force of only two men.

There were five districts, served by J. K. Glover, S. Woodbury, D. L. Kennedy, J. W. Mills, and W. L. Murphy.

The bishop kindly relieved me from the district and placed me on the Gainesville and Micanopy Circuit, with E. H. Giles as junior preacher. This year the civil war began, and the Church in all its operations sympathized with the excitement. Congregations were everywhere decimated, companies and regiments forming everywhere. Many of our ministers were accepting chaplaincies, others rushing to the front as officers or soldiers. A company of cavalry was formed, consisting mostly of my neighbors and former students, to go to Fernandina. They urged me to go with them as chaplain. After consultation with my charge, the deep interest I felt in the men, with a hope that a change to the coast might improve my wife's health, induced me to accept.

In Fernandina I found myself independent chaplain (for I was not commissioned, but was supported by the company) of from two thousand five hundred to four thousand soldiers, besides acting pastor of all the congregations in the city. For most of the time I was there I was the only minister engaged in that work on the island. My congregations of course were large, and I had plenty of preaching to do. Visiting and ministering to the sick and burying the dead was the hardest part of my work.

My own health failed. I had mumps, followed by typhoid fever, terminating in camp flux, so in about six months after entering the service, and while camping in the woods after the evacuation of Fernandina, my surgeon said to me: "My kind advice to you is, go home and get well if you can; and if not, die among your friends, for it is absolutely impossible for you to get well in the army." No one who has not passed through a similar experience can conceive of the sadness of that hour. To leave these men who had shown such appreciation of my services, and had treated me with such respect and kindness, to contemplate future diseases, wounds, and all the horrors of war, with no one to point them to a Saviour or offer a prayer by their dying bed, seemed almost too much for me; yet a Power beyond myself seemed to point out the path of duty, so I returned to my home in Micanopy and spent the remaining Sabbaths of the year, whenever able and opportunity offered, going to different camps and preaching to the soldiers, and otherwise filling appointments within my reach.

Though the year 1861 was one of great trials to the Church, our records show an increase of five hundred and ninety-one white and two hundred and sixty-one colored members.

Two of our ministers died. D. D. Henry, a man of deep piety and sterling worth, fell at his post on the Suwannee Circuit in September. S. E. Randolph, who, moved by the impulse of patriotism, entered the army, went to Virginia, but in three months death claimed him for its victim.

The eighteenth session of our Conference met in Quincy, December 12, 1861, Bishop Pierce presiding, and P. P. Smith, Secretary.

W. W. Anthony was the only one admitted; J. J.

Sealey was readmitted; O. L. Smith and N. B. Ousley were received by transfer; two had died and one located; five of us were in the Confederate army, and two were transferred from us.

This was the first Annual Conference I had ever failed to attend. The districts remained the same, except S. Woodbury was placed on the Tallahassee District in place of J. K. Glover, whose health had failed, and R. H. Luckey on the Thomasville District.

Though the Church was passing through fiery trials, she still held her own with a net increase of two hundred and fifty-five white and two hundred and seven colored members.

Our Conference held its nineteenth session in Tallahassee, December 11, 1862, Bishop Andrew presiding, and P. P. Smith, Secretary.

George B. Swan was admitted, and J. G. Worley readmitted; James T. Stockton, J. Rast, and J. Henderson located; our superannuate and supernumerary lists embraced fifteen men, six were in the army, and C. W. Parker and B. J. Johnson removed by transfer; three had passed away by death.

This large decrease in our membership, the general state of the country, the disorganized condition of the Church by the absence of nearly all the white men in the army, called upon those who remained for more than ordinary faith. But with faith in God our Conference work was completed.

The districts remained the same, except Jacksonville, which was served by J. M. Hendry in place of J. W. Mills, who had gone into the army as chaplain.

This year was one of general discouragement, the large decrease in ministerial force, the fact that nearly all who remained were compelled to engage in some secular employment to supplement their support to the point of actual necessity, and the state of the country at large, caused a decrease of three hundred and fifty-seven white and nine hundred and eighty-seven colored members. The roll call of deaths this year was also heavy.

Peyton P. Smith was a leading member of the Conference from its organization, having previously traveled twelve years under the direction of the Georgia Conference while it embraced Florida. At the time of our organization he was presiding elder of the Tallahassee District. From then to the close of his life he filled important positions. He carried close system into everything he touched. He kept a voluminous diary, from which we learn that he was a preacher for thirty years and four months, that he preached four thousand four hundred and fourteen sermons, made five thousand nine hundred and seventy-nine visits, wrote four thousand nine hundred and forty-one letters, traveled almost entirely by private conveyance one hundred and three thousand six hundred and twenty-three miles. He was tall and slender, had a broad though low forehead, and when animated had a piercing eye. His sermons were always systematic, and generally doctrinal. His descriptive powers were good, and when bordering on the awful he became almost overwhelming. Who that ever heard him preach when deeply moved, from the text, "Therefore will I number you to the sword," can ever forget the impression made? His last illness was short, his end triumphant.

John J. Richards was a man of fervent spirit, a

fine singer, a good preacher, and a faithful laborer. He died of cancer, in Madison, after having served the Church twenty-four years, being forty-six years of age.

Joseph A. W. Johnson was a member of the Conference seven years. Earnest and faithful, he was loved in every charge he served. But consumption severed the silver cord, and in his early manhood transferred him from his earthly prison to the palace of his God.

CHAPTER VIII.

From 1863 to 1866.

THE twentieth session of our Conference met in Thomasville December 16, 1863, Bishop Andrew presiding; F. A. Branch, Secretary. Here we admitted Alfred Holcombe, D. L. Branning, W. A. McLean, and A. T. Hollyman.

A. Holcombe traveled two years, discontinued, and settled in Orange County, serving the Church as a useful local preacher.

David L. Branning was a young man of fine natural abilities, a good academic education, a fine singer, and faithful worker. He traveled a few years; then the cares of a large family, and the meager support growing out of the condition of the country, caused him to locate. He lives in Waldo, highly respected, a local preacher, and a faithful worker.

W. A. McLean was a young man of fine education, a good preacher, and faithful worker, but the necessities of his family caused his early location. He went to Jacksonville and practiced law. For many years he served as Judge of Probate, and is always ready to preach and work for the Church.

A. T. Hollyman was also a young man of fine preaching abilities, a useful man, but soon passed to the local ranks. When I last saw him he was still doing good work as a local preacher.

Though the Conference had encouragement in the admission of these young men, still the war cloud lowered, society was disorganized, and the general prospect was far from encouraging. Few changes were made, and the preachers returned to meet whatever changes might await them. I was sent to Alachua Colored Mission; but owing to the fact of Rev. T. A. Carruth leaving our Church and joining the Presbyterian, I was changed to the Micanopy Circuit at our first quarterly meeting.

Our Conference held its twenty-first session at Monticello December 14, 1864. Rev. S. P. Richardson was elected President, and F. A. Branch, Secretary. John M. Potter and J. O. A. Sparks were admitted. Thomas H. Capers and Marshal G. Jenkins readmitted. Henry D. Moore was received by transfer. James G. Acton located. Henry F. Smith, Leroy B. Giles, R. W. Burgess, David L. Kennedy, Amos Davis, and John P. Urquhart had died.

The white men of our State were nearly all in the Confederate army.

Three of our members were sent as missionaries to the soldiers, and the rest were sent to the various fields of labor within our bounds. But nearly all of these were compelled to supplement their small salaries by some secular occupation.

Of our comrades that had fallen during the year, we only state that Henry F. Smith embraced religion when quite young, joined our Conference in 1856, rendered eight years of efficient service, was earnest but not morose, fell at his post saying as he passed away: "All is well."

Leroy B. Giles joined our Church when quite young, was admitted into our Conference in 1856, spent the remainder of his life in faithful, useful, and loving labor, sweetly passing away in peace.

R. W. Burgess, formerly of the South Carolina Conference, was readmitted in Micanopy in 1860. Though not brilliant, he was deeply spiritual, earnest, and useful. His end was peace.

David L. Kennedy was converted while young; began his ministerial work in Tennessee, and was transferred to us in 1855. He possessed fine intellectual powers, and during the nine years of service to our Conference his advancement was rapid. He had a pleasing address, a consecrated heart, and a life of usefulness.

Amos Davis rendered ten years of faithful service to the Conference, and passed to his reward in holy triumph.

John F. Urquhart rendered the Conference but four years' service, but his earnest zeal won many seals to his ministry. Several years ago, the now sainted Corly, of Georgia, told me that Urquhart was his spiritual father. He described the scene of the young missionary going to his camp during the war, preaching to the soldiers, then wrestling in prayer with the young officer until he found peace. I replied to him that our young brother was taken from us early, yet he still preaches through you, and you will doubtless leave some one to pass the word down through the ages. "Yes," said he; "no minister has a right to die until he has consecrated his successor."

The twenty-second session of our Conference was held in Madison November 29, 1865, Bishop Pierce presiding, and F. A. Branch, Secretary.

No pen, much less mine, could draw a picture of this Conference session. Since our last, the bloody civil war had closed, and the remainder of the armies returned to their desolate homes. Half a million of graves from the two armies marked the desolation of war. There was scarcely a family that had not been decimated by its ravages. The whole system of labor was crushed, currency destroyed, plantations desolated, and political disabilities heaped upon us, while home itself was insecure.

With many misgivings the preachers had left their homes to attend Conference. We scarcely dared contemplate the future. How could we meet the actual necessities of wives and children and yet serve the Church, when that Church was bankrupt in purse and almost despairing in mind? But the crisis was met with a living faith. The work was rearranged, as far as possible, to meet the necessities of the case.

W. S. Rice was admitted. J. R. Harold and G. C. Andrews located. W. L. Murphy had been called to his reward. He was a native of Ireland; had begun his ministerial career in the Baltimore Conference in 1846; for a number of years had been a member of our Conference, a devout Christian, an able minister, and a gentleman in all the relations of life.

This year I was sent to Leon Circuit and colored charge. This charge embraced the largest colored population of any in our bounds. The new relation to the freedmen involved very delicate responsibilities. Previously our Church had spent large amounts for "missions to people of color." In addition to this, each minister was required to give one service each Sunday to them. We had also made special arrangements, for all who desired to do so, to worship with the whites in all our churches. Hence we had a large colored membership all over the South.

But now with a change of circumstances there must be a change of operations. It was utterly impossible for us to keep up our missions; still we tried to render them all the service possible, and could we have served them with the whites, until they could have ministers of their own color, at least partially educated, it would have been better for them. But the perfect flood of what was known as "carpetbaggers," in their endeavors to obtain power and wealth for themselves by the votes of the enfranchised freedmen, so operated upon them that before the close of this year most of them had withdrawn from our communion. We, however, continued to serve them wherever practicable, and during the year preached, generally to large congregations.

Our Conference held its twenty-third session in Quincy December 13, 1866, Bishop McTyeire presiding, and F. A. Branch, Secretary. Nathan Talley and earnest Crum were admitted. R. H. Rogers was readmitted. James P. De Pass was received by transfer. Our reports showed a decrease of seven hundred and fifty-nine whites and two thousand five hundred and five colored members.

The General Conference had divided the Georgia Conference, and put all our territory in that State into the South Georgia Conference. This took from us nearly half our territory and involved the transfer of nearly half of our members. By this means we lost from our roll J. M. Hendry, M. G. Jenkins, J. W. Simmons, S. G. Childs, C. P. Jones, M. H. Fielding, J. D. Maulden, Nathan Talley, O. L. Smith,

James Harris, J. W. Mills, W. A. Parks, R. H. Howren, R. M. Flournoy, O. B. Stanley, W. M. Kennedy, R. F. Evans, H. D. Moore, J. M. Potter, J. G. Worley, J. M. N. Lowe, and C. P. Jones.

The following tells of those removed by death during the year:

Thomas H. Capers was the son of Gabriel Capers, and nephew of Bishop Capers. He was born in South Carolina in 1811, entered the Georgia Conference when nineteen years of age, located in 1846, was readmitted into the Florida Conference in 1864, and died in Monticello October 15, 1866. He was a polished gentleman, a zealous laborer, and an earnest Christian.

Francis M. Wilson, at the time of his death, was nearly thirty-three years of age. At seventeen he was converted, and five years afterwards entered the ministry. His faith was strong, he labored zealously eleven years, and peacefully passed to his reward.

Mahlon Bedell was born in North Carolina in 1806. He embraced religion and entered the ministry in South Carolina when quite young, where he remained some years. He gave the remnant of his days to Georgia and Florida. "Blessed are the dead that die in the Lord."

This year I served the Gadsden Circuit.

CHAPTER IX.

From 1867 to 1876.

Our Conference held its twenty-fourth session in Monticello, beginning December 6, 1867, Bishop Pierce in the chair, and F. A. Branch, Secretary.

In some respects this was a sad Conference to the members. From year to year we had been called upon to see here and there a vacant seat in our body. But now nearly half our number were gone, most of whom we should see no more in the flesh. The territory rendered dear to many of us by years of toil, no longer ours, the missions which under God we had raised to stations and circuits, now belonged to another Conference. Although these are but the outcome of progress, and necessary to the further development of the work, yet the change means the severing of many sacred ties.

After the work had been arranged we had four districts, the number with which we started twenty-three years ago. We had thirty-six effective men, only five more than we had then. Four of these were just admitted—viz., W. McKay, T. K. Leonard, C. H. Bernheim, and E. J. Knight.

We rejoiced in the fact that none of our number had been called away by death. Our minutes show an increase of four hundred and twelve white and a decrease of nine hundred and seventeen colored members.

W. F. Easterling, James B. Jackson, W. E. Collier, and T. W. Moore were appointed to the districts. I was sent to Micanopy.

Our Conference held its twenty-fifth session in Jacksonville, beginning January 13, 1869, Bishop Wightman, President, and F. A. Branch, Secretary. We admitted on trial J. H. D. McRae and George C. Level. We reported increase of whites, three hundred and one; decrease of colored, eighty-one. The collections for the year had been: Conference collections, $625; domestic missions, $318.15; foreign missions, $135. We lost by transfer F. R. C. Ellis and W. H. Thomas; by death, James B. Jackson and William McKay.

James B. Jackson was a remarkable man. Until fourteen years of age he did not know that he had seen a Bible. About this time the children of the family where he was working taught him his letters. One of them gave him a Testament, which was then his first and only book. This he spelled through. Soon he was teaching school, was converted and shortly entered the ministry, which he faithfully served for over thirty years. He filled important places both in Georgia and Florida. He died in perfect peace in Lake City February 18, 1868. His death was caused by a railroad accident at Baldwin.

William McKay was a native of Scotland. In early life his family came to America and settled in Rome, Ga. He entered the army and was wounded. He was a faithful Christian in or out of the army. In 1868 he entered his eternal rest from the Ancilla Mission, where he was serving his second year.

The twenty-sixth session of our Conference met in Lake City December 20, 1869, Bishop Doggett in the chair, and J. P. De Pass, Secretary. T. W. Tomkies, R. H. Barnett, S. E. Philips, and U. S. Bird were admitted. M. A. Clonts was readmitted, and Oliver Eady was received by transfer. C. P. Murdock located. J. O. A. Sparks had been called to rest. He was a man of intellect, a natural orator. He had preached in Georgia two years, had served Gainesville, Fla., two years, and at our last Conference he was sent to Key West, where he fell at his post, a martyr to yellow fever, May 15. His end was peace.

The Conference held its twenty-seventh session in Tallahassee, beginning January 4, 1871, Bishop Wightman presiding, and U. S. Bird, Secretary. D. W. Core, J. W. Barnett, S. Moore, R. M. Ellzey, and J. Rast were admitted. J. J. Sealey, C. P. Murdock, and S. A. McCook were readmitted. J. M. Stokes and W. Jerdone were received by transfer. W. W. Hicks was received from the Lutheran Church. J. W. Jackson and D. L. Branning located. R. I. McCook had been removed by death. He had served the Church faithfully for a number of years, and died in peace in Key West. W. W. Hicks was removed by transfer.

Our reports showed an increase of one thousand six hundred and sixty white, and a decrease of two hundred and ninety-six colored members. The districts remained the same, and were served by A. J. Wooldrich, J. A. Wiggins, J. P. De Pass, and E. F. Gates. I was returned to Micanopy.

Our Conference met for its twenty-eighth session in Madison January 3, 1872, Bishop Wightman presiding, and U. S. Bird, Secretary. Henry E. Partridge was admitted. C. A. Fulwood, A. A. Robinson, and W. R. Johnson were received by transfer. C. P. Murdock located. A. J. Wooldrich and Thomas Taylor had been removed by death.

A. J. Wooldrich was a polished shaft, genial, loving, polite, and earnest. He never forgot the smallest point in the life of a gentleman. He filled some of our most important fields. He loved every one, and was loved by all.

Thomas Taylor was a plain, practical man. He was an old man when he entered the Conference, faithfully served for several years, passed to the superannuate list, and in 1872 peacefully passed to his reward.

This year our districts were reduced to three, and were served by J. A. Wiggins, J. P. De Pass, and E. H. Giles.

This year my health was somewhat feeble; and this, with other considerations, caused me to ask a superannuate relation. I did so with many misgivings, and was never satisfied with it. Though, during the two years I held that relation, I preached nearly as much and tried to serve the Church as faithfully as if I had been in charge of a pastorate. And here I would record, with thankfulness, that, although never strong, yet I have not been prevented by sickness during the last twenty-five years, from filling my regular appointments an average of one sermon for each Sunday in the year. And now (1897), though near seventy-five years of age, I can preach two or three times a day without special inconvenience. To God be all the glory.

Our Conference held its twenty-ninth session in Fernandina January 8, 1873, Bishop Marvin presiding, and U. S. Bird, Secretary. J. S. Collier and J. D. Rogers were admitted. J. M. Bridges was readmitted. C. D. Nicholson and G. Bright were received by transfer. J. Rast located. The returns showed a decrease of one hundred and twenty-seven white and seven colored members. T. K. Leonard, L. G. R. Wiggins, E. B. Duncan, W. K. Turner, and U. S. Bird left us by transfer.

Our thirtieth session met in Jacksonville January 7, 1874, Bishop Pierce presiding, and F. Pasco, Secretary.

J. E. A. Vanduzer, R. Martin, W. H. F. Roberts, A. A. Barnett, J. D. McDonell, S. D. Robinson, McK. F. McCook, and T. J. Philips were admitted. J. P. Fitzpatrick, R. H. Howren, and W. F. Lewis were received by transfer. There were no locations nor deaths.

Our increase of members was two hundred and twenty-eight whites and twenty colored.

Another district was formed. The districts were served by S. Woodbury, A. A. Robinson, T. W. Moore, and J. J. Sealey.

I was sent to Micanopy and Gainesville Circuit. This year we built a church in Gainesville. We had at first preached in the courthouse; after the Presbyterians completed their house they kindly offered us its use one Sunday in the month, but after years of labor we still saw but little fruits to our church. This year we resolved to have a house of worship of our own. But the observer of the present day can hardly conceive of what that undertaking involved. With between twenty and thirty members, all poor, and with very small income, it required strong faith to begin the work. But the lot was given by the county commissioners. Mr. Grissom agreed to superintend the work for nothing, if money was furnished weekly to pay the mechanics. The lumber was secured, and then came the "tug of war." The carpenters had to be paid every week. The ladies worked, walked the streets, and begged from all they met, Jew or Gentile, saint or sinner. Though often discouraged, "faint yet pursuing," they never rested until the building was completed and furnished. Great was our joy when we entered our own place of worship. A Sabbath school and prayer meeting was organized the same day. And now, looking back over the past twenty-three years, I see the laborers of that day, all at work, *all the time* at work, until the "capstone is brought forth with shouting and praise." Among the foremost of that band stands Mr. Grissom, Rev. O. A. Myers, Capt. Crawford, Mrs. Myers, Mrs. McCall, Mrs. G. P. Thomas, Mrs. McKinstrey, Mrs. R. Y. H. Thomas, and J. C. Gardner. From that time until now our progress has been marked, and to-day we can but exclaim: "What hath God wrought!"

Our Conference held its thirty-first session in Live Oak December 16, 1874, Bishop Wightman presiding, and F. Pasco, Secretary.

W. Robertson and J. A. Castel were admitted. M. M. Michean, T. A. Carruth, A. Peeler, and J. M. Hendry were readmitted. W. W. Hicks, C. E. Dowman, O. W. Ransom, and R. D. Gentry were received by transfer. J. M. Bridges and T. A. Carruth located. W. F. Lewis was removed by transfer, and George Bright by death. He was a man of good academic education, a strong reasoner, perhaps a little too fond of controversy. He had been in the itineracy about twenty-four years, only two of which were spent in Florida. He died in Key West of yellow fever September 20, 1874.

Our reports showed an increase of one thousand and fifty-two white and nine colored members, also an increase in value of churches of $13,400, and of parsonages of $4,710.

I was returned to Micanopy and Gainesville.

Our Conference held its thirty-second session in Quincy, beginning January 5, 1876, Bishop Wightman presiding, and F. Pasco, Secretary.

H. F. Philips and G. W. Mitchell were admitted. W. G. Boothe was readmitted. H. B. Frazer, W. C. Collins, J. H. Johnson, W. F. Norton, and W. M. Watts were received by transfer. C. D. Nicholson and W. W. Hicks located. J. Anderson was removed by transfer, and J. M. Stokes, S. A. McCook, and J. E. A. Vanduzer were removed by death.

James M. Stokes was a man of very feeble health, yet possessed wonderful pathos and fervent piety. Though engaged several years in the ministry, his health enabled him to do but few years of regular work, two only of which were in Florida. He died in Live Oak April 19, 1875, beloved by his brethren and in perfect peace with his God.

S. A. McCook was a native of Georgia. He entered the Conference in 1852, where he labored until 1861. He was readmitted in 1871. In three years his health failed, and July 7, 1875, he peacefully breathed his last.

J. E. A. Vanduzer was a native of New York. He was admitted into our Conference in January, 1871, and was sent as a missionary to the Cubans in Key West, where he died of yellow fever June 7, 1875. His stay with us was short, but his lovely spirit and fervent piety caused him to be loved by all. His last words were: "Tell the Conference not to give up the Cuban Mission."

This year I was sent to organize Orange Lake Mission. We organized a church at Millwood, since which time they built a church, and about 1891 they removed the society and built a nice church on the railroad at Reddick. They have since built a parsonage and made this the headquarters of the Reddick Circuit. Another appointment was Cabbage Hammock, where we received a number of members and organized a church which has since been removed to Citra and is now a flourishing station. Another appointment was Spring Hill, which has since been removed to Anthony, where a good church and parsonage have been built. This is now the headquarters of the Anthony Circuit.

The year was one of much pleasure to the pastor, and we trust of good to the people.

CHAPTER X.

From 1877 to 1880.

THE thirty-third session of our Conference met in Monticello January 11, 1877, Bishop Pierce presiding, and F. Pasco, Secretary.

Having been unable to procure the minutes for this session, we simply state that J. B. Ley with others was admitted. I was sent to Key West,.first charge, where I remained four years. This charge included the superintendency of our Cuban Mission. H. B. Someillan was the missionary. On reaching my charge I soon realized that if anything of importance was done for the Cuban work we *must* have a place of worship for them. On looking around I found a very eligible site for a church, with an almost new house on it. The owner wanted to leave the city, and offered the property at a very low price (one thousand two hundred and fifty dollars). I saw that for seven hundred and fifty dollars the house could be remodeled and made into a chapel sufficient to accommodate our congregation, and in a central position for the Cuban population. Meeting Bishop Pierce at Manatee in the spring, I laid the whole matter before him. He promised his help to raise one thousand dollars from the missionary society, and we began the tedious work of raising the remainder. The lot was finally purchased and paid for, the house remodeled and furnished, and our Cuban brethren moved into their own premises. It is true the house was not altogether such a one as we could have desired, but the auditorium was neat and capable of seating some three hundred people. It also gave to our Cuban work a home and habitation, from which our present work among the Cubans has developed.

During these years Rev. H. B. Someillan rendered faithful work to the mission. Rev. A. Silvera and Miss Pyfrom conducted a school which wielded a good influence upon the children. Rev. S. Gardener, a former pastor of our Church in Key West, had been, perhaps, the first to preach to them from our Church there. Rev. C. A. Fulwood followed, and during his pastorate Mr. Vanduzer was sent as missionary to the Cubans. He was succeeded by Mr. Diaz, a whole-souled, spiritual man, who had wonderful influence with the Cubans. He circulated literature, prayed, and preached, and during his brief ministry there were nearly one hundred names added to our Church. But the adding of names to the Church roll we found to be the easiest part of our work. I will illustrate. A Cuban arrives in the city and is told there is a Methodist Church there. Curiosity prompts him to go out and see for himself. The church is pointed out. To one accustomed to magnificent cathedrals, patronized by the State and ornamented by the gifts of the wealthy for centuries, our little chapel, without spire, bell, or ornaments, seems very insignificant. But he enters, sees a minister rise, sing, pray, and preach. At the simple story of the cross the tear starts in his eye. Services closed, he meets the missionary in the aisle, and says: "I like your service, I want to join your Church." But undertake to expound a spiritual regeneration to him, and you will find that he thinks he was made a Christian when he was baptized, and to urge the necessity of the new birth only evokes the question: "How can these things be?"

But the difficulty and triumph in some of these cases may be understood by the experience of one man. Having struggled with these questions long and earnestly, he said: "I finally realized that man has a body, which is material; he also has a soul, which is spiritual; water is material. Now the application of water, which is material, to my body, which is material, can never remove the sins from my soul, which is spiritual." Then, tearing loose from the mere ordinance of the Church, he found peace through faith in Christ alone.

I often preached to the Cubans through an interpreter, and wrote sermons which were translated and read to them by the missionary. But I must leave them and come to my special charge.

The population of the city at that time was estimated at sixteen thousand, roughly estimated at one-third Bahaians and their descendants, one-third Cubans, and one-third negroes, with some natives of different parts of the United States, and some from nearly all parts of the world.

My congregation with its following was about one thousand, nearly three hundred of whom were members of the Church and between four and five hundred members of the Sabbath school. Our church had been estimated to seat eight hundred persons, but we found it too small to seat the congregation. Besides it had been standing for over thirty years, was fearfully out of repair, and was considered by many unsafe for a large congregation. The style was antiquated, and while many thought we could not build a new house, the sentiment was general not to spend money on the old one. After many consultations a plan was adopted near the close of my first year, and the corner stone was laid. The building was to be of stone quarried upon the island, and the work was to proceed only as we had money in hand to pay as the work progressed. The collection of funds was committed to the pastor, and we found that to raise funds each week to pay for the work of the week gave him plenty of practice in walking. But during the three years we raised and paid on it over five thousand dollars, finished the wall of the first story, put on a temporary covering, and began worshiping in it.

The plan after I left was finally changed, the congregation becoming discouraged in regard to carrying out the original design, and finished it up as a one-story building.

During our stay in Key West we passed through two epidemics of yellow fever, but, thanks be to God! while we were severely and dangerously afflicted, none of us died. Many hallowed associations cluster around the memory of our home on that "seagirt isle." Many loved ones have crossed the flood, which makes the hope of heaven sweeter.

CHAPTER XI.

From 1877 to 1883.

THE Conference held its thirty-fifth session in Gainesville, beginning November 3, 1878, Bishop Kavanaugh presiding, and F. Pasco, Secretary. T. J. Nixson, W. S. Richardson, A. W. J. Best, W. M. McIntosh, and F. R. Bridges were admitted on trial. T. A. Carruth was readmitted. W. O. Butler, N. Z. Glenn, W. Shockley, and P. T. Mann were received by transfer. J. T. Neel, E. H. Giles, and R. D. Gentry located. N. Z. Glenn and J. B. McFarland were removed by transfer. George W. Fagg, E. B. Duncan, S. B. Smitteel, and E. W. Woodbury died.

George W. Fagg had spent many years in the work earnestly and successfully. He loved every one, and they in turn loved him.

E. B. Duncan was an old man, and had given a long life to the work, several years of which he labored as missionary among the Indians. He finished his course in peace.

S. B. Smitteel was a faithful and useful man. His dust rests in hope.

E. W. Woodbury was a bright and earnest young man, but before the bud was matured it was transplanted to bloom by the river of life.

Our Conference held its thirty-sixth session in Tallahassee, beginning December 17, 1879, Bishop Doggett in the chair, and F. Pasco, Secretary.

W. S. Armistead, W. Dunbar, J. B. Johnston, M. A. Philips, and A. M. C. Russell were admitted. R.

M. Tydings, James Atkins, and C. H. Ford were received by transfer. Isaac Mundane and George C. Leavel had been called to their reward.

They had been earnest and spiritual laborers, and passed peacefully to their everlasting rest.

Our thirty-seventh session of the Conference convened in Ocala December 16, 1880, Bishop Pierce presiding, and F. Pasco, Secretary.

R. B. Bryan, S. B. Black, O. A. Hiscock, L. W. Moore, and T. A. Branch were admitted. H. B. Avery was received by transfer. H. T. Philips, T. A. Carruth, and C. H. Ford located.

I was sent to Marion Circuit. The work had no parsonage, consequently I lived at my home at Micanopy. This required long rides each week, but we received a cordial welcome, and spent this and the following years pleasantly and, I trust, profitably.

Near the close of the second year arrangements were made for building a parsonage, which was accomplished the following year.

The thirty-eighth session of our Conference convened in Monticello January 18, 1882, Bishop McTyeire presiding, and F. Pasco, Secretary.

E. J. Holmes, W. H. Steinmyer, W. F. Le Gette, A. Silvera, and E. F. Ley were admitted. E. H. Giles was readmitted. R. L. Honiker, E. H. Harmon, H. H. Kennedy, A. C. Le Gette, and W. A. Simmons were received by transfer. S. A. Carson, T. W. Moore, and W. M. McIntosh located. W. G. Royster had died.

He had been a faithful minister, earnest and devoted. He insisted earnestly on the execution of every point of our discipline, great and small.

Our Conference held its thirty-ninth session in Jacksonville January 3, 1883, Bishop Kavanaugh presiding, and F. Pasco, Secretary.

A. O. Baker, J. H. D. McRae, James Russell, C. W. Morrison, W. R. Reasonover, M. H. Outland, J. G. Graham, J. F. Shands, J. C. Pace, and T. A. Branch were admitted. J. W. Hannah, Jr., T. S. Armistead, J. S. Smith, P. L. Smith, and P. A. Murray were received by transfer.

Our death record this year was large: T. R. Barnett, E. J. Hughes, J. A. Wiggins, S. L. Smith, and H. B. Avery.

T. R. Barnett was one of our aged men, had served the Church long and acceptably and with much usefulness. He leaves to the Church many spiritual children and two sons who are earnest laborers and useful ministers in our Conference.

J. A. Wiggins was a man of power who had rendered much service to the Church, both in Georgia and Florida.

S. L. Smith, young, educated, prudent, spiritual, and lovely, was called in his young manhood from labor to rest.

H. B. Avery, though feeble in health, was strong intellectually and spiritually. His work was well done; he rests in peace.

CHAPTER XII.

From 1884 to 1889.

OUR Conference held its fortieth session in Madison, commencing January 14, 1884, Bishop Keener presiding, and F. Pasco, Secretary.

S. S. Gasque, T. J. Evans, George Lee, T. M. White, O. W. Collier, J. Russell, R. Storke, and E. B. Pooser were admitted on trial. W. R. Reasonover, J. C. Pace, and O. A. Hiscock were discontinued. John Penny, O. W. Ransom, and W. O. Hampton had died.

John Penny was a Scotchman. He was impulsive and often expressed his feelings roughly, yet had a kind heart, and was always ready to forgive and ask forgiveness whenever there was occasion. He was one of our original members, and did much hard frontier work in the early years of our Conference. But in his young manhood he was attacked with throat trouble, and was compelled to spend the remainder of his years upon the superannuated list.

O. W. Ransom came to us from the Tennessee Conference. He was at that time in very feeble health, and came hoping to find relief in our climate; but consumption finished its work in a few years, and he peacefully fell asleep.

W. A. Hampton rendered us a few years of faithful and useful work, and passed triumphantly to his rest.

The forty-first session of our Conference met in

Gainesville January 7, 1885, Bishop Parker presiding, and F. Pasco, Secretary.

G. W. Kennedy, R. O. Weir, W. A. Brown, R. M. Evans, L. W. Browder, and J. E. Neal were admitted. J. W. McCrary was readmitted. A. E. Householder, W. F. Alexander, B. E. Ledbetter, and J. S. Duncan were received by transfer. A. C. Le Gette and A. Silvera located. J. F. Shands, M. H. Outland, O. W. Collier, E. B. Pooser, and T. A. Branch were discontinued. C. W. Morrison, having been expelled, was discontinued by the Conference. Edwin L. Smith and J. J. Sealey had passed to their reward.

E. L. Smith was earnest and faithful, and was cut down in the very bud of usefulness.

J. J. Sealey had been in the work for many years, had served districts, stations, and circuits, and was always successful. His spirit was sweet, his work earnest. He rests from his labors.

Our Conference held its forty-second session in Orlando, beginning January 6, 1886, Bishop Hargrove presiding, and F. Pasco, Secretary.

The weather was excessively cold, and marked an era in our State. The orange industry had become our chief source of income, especially in the east and south. But this freeze threw this back so as to cripple the finances of our State for years.

At this Conference W. J. Dowell, D. A. Cole, W. J. Gray, A. O. Hiscock, C. W. Inman, J. N. Jones, W. J. Morris, F. Pixton, T. B. Reynolds, R. Storke, J. A. Giddens, and C. J. Williams were admitted.

The Conference took steps for the publication of a Conference paper. Rev. J. P. De Pass was elected editor, if the committee should succeed in making arrangements for its publication. The arrangements were soon made, and the editor elect was called to the tripod, and in Sanford our *Florida Christian Advocate* made its appearance, and continues (1897) to pay weekly visits to all who desire its society.

I had been appointed Sunday School Agent, but was changed to the Bronson Circuit by the presiding elder to fill the place made vacant by the removal of Mr. De Pass. Here we passed a pleasant year, renewing old acquaintances and forming new ones. The preaching services were not hard, though the traveling in buggy was. As there was no parsonage on the work, the pastor had to live at his home in Micanopy and serve the circuit from there. We had, however, a pleasant and, I think, successful year. There were numbers of accessions, and a good church built in Bronson.

Our Conference held its forty-third session in Tallahassee December 16-21, 1886, Bishop Hendrix presiding, and F. Pasco, Secretary.

A. H. Gibbons, J. M. Sweat, J. W. Porter, J. Belton, J. S. Barnett, H. A. H. Crompton, and W. S. McMannin were admitted.

The author was sent to Cedar Keys Station, a small city on the Gulf at the western terminus of the F. C. and P. railroad. There was no church nor parsonage here. I rented a part of a house, and began the work of the three following years. The Methodists, Presbyterians, and Baptists all worshiped in the basement of the schoolhouse. The membership of each was small. The room was too small for the congregation, and very inconvenient. And withal we were "tenants at will." Any day the school committee might need their premises and leave us without a place of worship.

My son was stationed in Palatka at the time, and Bishop Hendrix had promised to go there and preach the dedication sermon of their new church. I went to meet him and consult him in regard to our work in Cedar Keys. He gave me much encouragement, promising his influence, that if we could secure the lot the Board would give us such assistance as would enable us to build. Returning, we secured the lot and began looking forward to our building. Soon after we began a daily prayer meeting, which was continued for nearly four weeks. All the Churches joined. Mr. Curry, from Gainesville, came to our assistance. My son also came from Palatka and helped us. The meeting resulted in over thirty accessions to our Church, about the same to the Presbyterian, and some to the Baptist and Episcopal Churches. During the same meeting we received a very liberal subscription to our church building, and soon began work. We finished a church costing about three thousand dollars, leaving very little debt, nearly all of which was to the Board of Church Extension. They gave us two hundred and fifty dollars, and loaned us the same amount.

We also felt the absolute necessity of a parsonage, and with the assistance of one hundred and fifty dollars given and the same amount loaned from the woman's branch of Church Extension we secured a good building near the church. A small debt was left on the parsonage, which has since been liquidated, as well as the debt upon the church.

I ought here to state that after the lines of railroads were completed to Tampa the line of travel has been diverted from here. This, with the closing of some of the mills, has reduced the population, so that (in 1897) it is not as large as when I was there. I should also state that during a storm (about 1894) a tidal wave struck Cedar Keys, and swept churches, dwellings, and everything in its track. Our church was totally wrecked, but is being rebuilt.

Before leaving Cedar Keys I ask the reader to indulge me in a personal note. On the 1st of December, 1889, I received a telegram, announcing the death, on that day, of my precious mother. She was nearly ninety-three years of age. She was in fairly good health, arose that morning and ate her breakfast as usual, lay down to rest, dropped off to sleep, and without a struggle or groan awoke with her Saviour. To that being, whose sacred influence watched over me in childhood, and was my safest counselor in riper years, I owe all the pleasures of earth and all my hopes of heaven. May I meet her "over there!"

CHAPTER XIII.

From 1888 to 1895.

OUR Conference held its forty-fourth annual session in Leesburg, beginning December 14, 1887, Bishop Key presiding, and F. Pasco, Secretary.

C. W. Braswell, I. S. Patterson, B. T. Rape, T. M. Strickland, W. W. Joiner, A. M. Dager, J. L. Rast, J. T. Bell, G. W. Sellers, W. J. Whiddon, G. W. Forrest, J. C. Pace, J. F. Shands, and S. Scott were admitted on trial.

At this Conference Rev. J. P. De Pass resigned the office of editor of the *Florida Christian Advocate*, and J. Anderson, D.D., succeeded him. Soon afterwards the house that was publishing the paper gave it up and refused to publish it any longer. However, he managed to keep it going until Conference. He was then elected editor and publisher of the paper, and has continued in that position until the present.

The Conference met for its forty-fifth session in Bartow January 9, 1889, Bishop Galloway presiding, and F. Pasco, Secretary.

J. A. Howland, William Scott, F. E. Shipp, D. T. McMullen, W. A. Brown, W. P. Hawkins, J. M. Perez, B. F. Mason, J. C. Sale, C. C. Temple, and E. V. Blackman were admitted. J. E. Penny and E. Wilson were readmitted. J. B. Anderson, F. M. Moore, I. A. Vernon, W. P. Hawkins, and J. M. Pike were received by transfer. J. T. Duncan located. J. R. Sharpe, J. L. M. Spain, and A. H.

Gibbons had died during the year. H. H. Kennedy, C. C. Thompson, E. H. Harmon, T. W. Dye, and W. M. McIntosh were removed by transfer.

Of those called to their reward, J. R. Sharpe was an earnest worker, and died at his post in Jacksonville, a victim to yellow fever.

Mr. Spain had been with us but a few years, yet long enough to gain the love of those with whom he labored.

A. H. Gibbons was a young man, just beginning his ministerial career. He was ardent, zealous, studious, and spiritual. His end was peace.

The forty-sixth session of our Conference met in Gainesville January 8, 1890, Bishop Keener in the chair, and F. Pasco, Secretary.

We admitted J. P. Abbott, J. A. White, J. B. Davis, Henry Hice, E. V. Blackman, T. H. Sistrunk, A. M. Mann, M. H. Outland, and C. A. Moya; by transfer, M. A. Philips, D. V. Price, T. G. Lang, J. A. White, J. H. Vann, and T. C. Bradford; discontinued, M. G. Perez and J. F. Bell; located, George Lee and C. A. Sanders. Death had taken from us W. J. Morris and R. H. Howren. C. L. Patillo was removed by transfer.

Mr. Morris was with us only a short time, having been paralyzed in his third year. He was a good man, "full of faith and the Holy Ghost."

Robert H. Howren was a veteran, falling at his post in the fiftieth year of itinerent career. He was one of the original members of our Conference, and had filled all classes of work, from mission to district, always acceptable, faithful, and useful. His end was triumphant.

The author was appointed to the Gainesville District at this Conference, which he served two years. It extended from Cedar Keys, Gainesville, and Melrose on the north to Pemberton's Ferry on the south, embracing twenty pastoral charges. My health was generally good, and I missed but two appointments on account of sickness during the two years. The pastors worked well, and blessings crowned their labors. Many were converted and added to the Church.

The connectional claims improved, and there was quite a revival in building and repairing churches and parsonages.

Among the churches built, we might mention a beautiful one at Archer, under the ministry of Rev. W. S. Richardson; another at Rockelle under W. C. Collins, and one finished at Micanopy, under J. P. Hilburn. A large and beautiful brick church was built in Ocala, under J. B. Ley. These years were passed pleasantly and, I trust, profitably to the work.

The forty-seventh session of our Conference convened in Monticello January 7, 1891, Bishop Duncan presiding, and F. Pasco, Secretary.

C. T. Blackburn, A. W. J. Best, A. O. Brown, C. S. Clariday, F. M. C. Eads, E. J. Gates, J. W. Henson, S. G. Madows, A. F. Pierce, S. W. Lawler, A. D. Penny, J. A. Riggs, C. M. Tillman, and E. K. Whiddon were admitted. H. T. Philips and R. M. Williams were readmitted. J. P. Hilburn, and J. T. Watts were received by transfer. H. W. Joiner located. M. A. Philips, D. V. Price, and F. M. Moore were removed by transfer. C. E. Pelot and R. M. Tydings were removed by death.

R. M. Tydings had been in the work nearly half

a century. He was intelligent, faithful, and beloved. His end was peace.

C. E. Pelot was comparatively young, and earnest, faithful, and spiritual. His life was a grand success, and his end was triumphant.

Our Conference held its forty-eighth session in Tampa, commencing January 6, 1892, Bishop Granberry presiding, and F. Pasco, Secretary.

C. B. Ames, W. B. Tresca, J. W. Brandford, G. W. Gatewood, J. L. Jones, W. A. Conoly, S. A. McCook, E. W. Barrington, J. A. Henry, A. S. Whedon, W. C. Norton, M. J. Perez, J. P. Durrance, and John Beers were admitted on trial. R. A. Holloway, F. A. Taylor, and D. D. Warwick were received by transfer. G. W. Forrest and O. A. Hiscock located. E. G. Chandler had died.

He was a man of lovely spirit, earnest, fervent, and thoroughly consecrated. He suffered much and lingered long, but ended his work in peace.

The forty-ninth session of our Conference met in Ocala January 4, 1893, Bishop Fitzgerald presiding, and F. Pasco, Secretary.

J. E. Mickler, E. W. Barrington, H. V. Penny, S. W. Walker, F. M. Dukes, and W. F. Melton were admitted. C. A. Saunders was readmitted. E. D. Cameron, J. Dodwell, A. A. Barnett, T. J. Philips, W. J. Dowell, and R. O. Weir were received by transfer. J. A. Giddens located. J. P. Abbott and S. A. McCook were discontinued, and H. J. H. Crumpton was expelled.

The year had been one of prosperity to our Church, and showed improvement in nearly all of its interests.

The fiftieth session of our Conference met in Palatka January 3, 1894, Bishop Haygood presiding, and F. Pasco, Secretary.

J. F. Bell, C. F. Mellor, A. D. Akin, H. F. Harris, H. Bush, W. A. Weir, and N. L. Wiggins were admitted on trial. G. W. Forrest and J. T. Coleman were readmitted. E. W. Barrington, T. A. Jordan, C. D. Ward, B. T. Rape, and J. W. Keithley were received by transfer. E. W. Barrington was discontinued. A. E. Pearce, A. O. Brown, C. C. Temple, and W. J. J. Whidden, located. A. A. Barnett, C. S. Bird, and A. Peeler had been removed by death.

A. A. Barnett had scarcely reached his meridian. He entered the ministry when eighteen years of age, and for nineteen years made full proof of the same. His sermons were systematic, clear, chaste, and deeply spiritual. Whether he served missions, circuits, stations, or districts, he was always beloved, and filled his charge usefully.

C. S. Bird was transferred to us in 1885, and made full proof of his work until called to his reward.

Dr. A. Peeler was one of the original members of our Conference, and was ordained elder at its first session. Part of his life was spent in the local ranks, and although useful there, his heart yearned for the regular pastorate, and he returned to spend his remaining strength in the service. He was a clear reasoner, and his sermons generally partook of a doctrinal type.

During this Conference the following resolution was adopted:

Whereas we have been brought in much and signal mercy

to the fiftieth session of the Florida Annual Conference, and it is good to remember the mercies, and praise Him from whom they come; be it

Resolved, That the Committee on Public Worship appoint a jubilee anniversary, selecting speakers and arranging a programme for the appropriate celebration of the semicentennial of the Florida Annual Conference.

This resolution was afterwards reconsidered, and the jubilee was postponed until our next session, and C. A. Fulwood, J. C. Ley, and T. W. Moore were appointed a committee to arrange for the same.

This brings us to the close of our first fifty years as a Conference, and to the opening of our fifty-first session, which met in Jacksonville January 9, 1895, Bishop Duncan presiding, and F. Pasco, Secretary.

We take from the minutes the following extract: "In compliance with a resolution of the last session of our Conference in January, 1894, that we hold a juibilee service in commemoration of the close of the fiftieth year since our organization as a Conference at Tallahassee in January, 1845 [February, 1845], the afternoon and night of Thursday, January 9, 1895, were devoted to said service. At 3 P.M. Rev. J. C. Ley, the only active member of the Conference who was present at the Tallahassee Conference, preached a sermon appropriate to the occasion. At night Rev. T. W. Moore, D.D., presided, and after appropriate religious services Rev. F. Pasco, Secretary, read a paper entitled 'The History of the Florida Conference by Decades.' Dr. Moore followed with a paper on 'The Darkest Period in the History of the Florida Conference.' Appropriate remarks were made by Rev. J. Anderson, D.D. Rev. F. A. Branch, a former member of the Conference, now of the South Georgia Conference, having arrived too late to take part in the exercises of Thursday, by request addressed the Conference on Saturday afternoon. A letter was read from Rev. E. L. T. Blake, D.D., a member of the Conference of 1845, now a superannuate, he being unable to attend."

Thus ended our jubilee service. Many sad and many glorious reminiscences were renewed. Many new and glorious vistas of coming triumphs dazzled the eyes of preachers and people. But these exercises closed, and so must all things of earth. Yet the thought of a final reunion animates us by the way.

CHAPTER XIV.

Conclusion.

AND now, dear reader, we approach the end of this humble volume. Should you say, "I am not satisfied with its contents," the author will reply in advance, "Neither am I." It has been written mostly while traveling circuits which required much riding, some of the time from necessity, to give part of my time to answering the questions for myself and family, "What shall we eat, what shall we drink, and wherewithal shall we be clothed?" leaving no means for traveling in search of records, and but little for the purchase of books for reference.

The book will show defects both in matter and manner, but perhaps it contains facts which may aid an abler pen in the future in producing a book of greater merit.

We have sadly passed over many names and incidents, with a brief sentence here and there, whose worth would require many pages to pay the tribute due. Many names appear with the brief notice of received and how disposed of, whose worth will only be revealed before the great white throne. But an attempt to do justice to all these would have swelled the volume far beyond the design of the author.

Again, the effort to embrace the essential facts connected with the different sessions of our Conference with the admission of members, etc., of course renders some parts monotonous. But these are important in their line, and may also render pleasure to some who read these pages, to find the name and date of admission of some whose memory they cherish, though the annals be ever so brief.

But I now propose to close these labors with one or two personal reminiscences. I place in an appendix two sermons preached by the author, and published by request, as they are on the same line and may add some interest to the volume. One was preached before the Conference at Gainesville January 11, 1885, while celebrating the Centennial of the organization of Methodism in America; the other before the Conference in Jacksonville January 10, 1895, on the celebration of the semicentennial of the organization of the Florida Conference.

And now, as a large part of my life has been spent in the saddle, I think it due the noble horse, the daily companion and friend of the Methodist itinerant, to give a brief notice to one of that noble race.

In the annals of 1846 I alluded to trading for a pony. His name was "Wilie;" and a more delightful saddle horse, with a few exceptions, was not to be found. He could live and keep fat where most horses would have starved, would eat almost anything from the kitchen or dairy, and bear his rider forty miles or more in the day so smoothly that many were the volumes read and the sermons studied while on his back. Many were the streams swam, with the feet of the rider on top of the saddle, reaching the opposite shore perfectly dry. But on one of these occasions, while the rider was thus perched up, he made a misstep which caused the saddlebags to rattle. Looking quickly and seeing the grotesque figure above him, he made a quick "right-about wheel," pitching the rider headforemost nearly to the bottom of the stream. On regaining my equilibrium I saw Wilie going up the hill from which he had come down. I saw my hat, umbrella, and saddlebags floating rapidly down the stream. Regaining these, I started for the retreating pony. But a run and walk of eight miles on a hot day through deep sand was necessary for the job. He would stop, eat grass, and wait until my hand was stretched forth to take the bridle; then, with the most provoking, fun-loving spirit, would kick up his heels, dash off a short distance and then resume his feeding as if nothing had happened. He made his way to the home of a friend, went into the lot, and patiently waited my arrival. I had prided myself upon my horsemanship, I had plenty of practice, and thought no horse could throw me. But I learned by experience that when he saw proper, and I was off my guard, he could place his head between his fore legs, kick so high that his back was nearly perpendicular, at the same time making so sudden a whirl that his head would be in the opposite direction, and as his heels came to the ground he found himself running and the parson found himself in an awkward pile in the road. But farewell, Wilie; I shall never look upon your like again.

I alluded in the annals of 1847 to fevers of the previous year. The rainy season of 1846 was the most copious of any that I have ever experienced. From day to day my clothes were drenched by the rain and dried by the sunshine. In June I was taken down with bilious fever in Tampa, where I remained ten days, much of the time more or less delirious. Getting a little better, against the advice of my physician I started to meet my appointments, but on reaching Brother Harn's (forty miles) I relapsed, and was unable to travel for several days. Remaining here until thinking I was able to travel, I started on my rounds, filled one appointment, and a chill came on before leaving the house. The next morning, feeling a little better, I started for my next appointment, but the fever soon rose until I knew not where I was. My faithful horse carried me to the home of Mr. Whitehurst, west of the Annuttaliga Hammock. Here I remained three weeks, feeling most of the time from day to day uncertain if I should live to see the next. Most of the family were down with fever. I did not expect to recover, but was not afraid of death; yet there was one thought that to me was terrible, to be buried there among strangers, far from the precious dust of loved ones. It took days of earnest struggling before I could say and feel: "The will of the Lord be done." But when that point was finally reached, such was the overflow of divine love and joy that with my remaining strength I shouted aloud the praises of God. From that time there was a turn for the better, and in due time I was again engaged in the loved employ of traveling, singing, and preaching the blessed gospel of my Saviour. But still I was subject to continued return of chills and fevers, until the following February, to which allusion has already been made.

And now, dear reader, if the perusal of these lines has given you pleasure and profit, I rejoice. And praying that you and I "may so pass the waves of this world, as finally to come to the land of everlasting rest," I bid you farewell.

APPENDIX.

CENTENARY OF METHODISM.*

The poor have the gospel preached to them. (Matt. xi. 5.)

WE present it as an axiomatic fact, that the gospel comes not to receive blessings, but to bless. In all merely human systems, the object of the originators is either personal advantage or the elevation of their system; hence their appeal is to wealth and power. Christianity, coming from a higher plane, simply stoops to earth for the purpose of blessing humanity, and as such reaches its hand first to the most needy and the most helpless. When the Son of God presents his credentials—credentials which are to command the faith of the world—he rests his whole claim to Messiahship upon six points, rising one above another to the grand climax of our text: "The blind receive their sight, and the lame walk, the lepers are cleansed, and the deaf hear, the dead are raised up, and the poor have the gospel preached to them."

Christ preaches to the poor; if Nicodemus receives his message, by it His name with honor is handed down the ages. If a rich man of Aramathea believes and embalms the Saviour's body, he embalms his own name with immortality. If Mary anoints her Lord with ointment, her name receives the odor of its fragrance and is wafted to the utmost bounds of time and space. Thus the Church comes to bless the world. No man is a necessity to the Church, but it is a necessity to every man; and the highest honors ever conferred upon a Newton, a Washington, a Wesley,

---

*A sermon delivered before the Florida Annual Conference January 11, 1885.

or a Stephens, were gathered at the foot of the cross. Then, with at least some degree of consciousness of the grandeur of Christ's Church and the frailty of man, we come to notice the one hundredth year of our existence as one branch of his Church in America.

But where is boasting? It is excluded. Could we present in one grand panorama, what God has done for the world during the past century, through the instrumentality of Methodism, we would fall upon our faces and adore, returning to him all the glory, and amidst the triumphant strains of praise would swell the chorus, still: "The poor have the gospel preached to them."

We now enjoy our first celebration of this kind, and it will be our last. Asbury and the heroes of 1784 are fallen asleep, and we occupy their places. If another service of this kind is ever held, it will be long after we are gathered to our fathers, and the third generation will be the actors. Then if this is our *first*—if this will be our last—how can we best improve it? Let us briefly review the past, survey the present, and, resting upon the promises and immutability of God, anticipate and prepare for future conquests.

I. THE PAST.

The true spirit of Christianity in every age has been to preach the gospel to the poor. This was the theme of Christ, of the apostles, of the early Church. Luther preached a free justification for the poor and awakened the pent up fires of ages, flashing their benign influence from the Mediteranean to the icebound regions of the North. A little less than one hundred and fifty years ago a company of devout students at Oxford united to search the Scriptures, pray, visit and preach to the poor, relieve distress as far as possible, and seek after personal holiness. Time will not permit us to dwell upon the struggles and triumphs of that little band; yet we cannot pass the eight or ten persons who in 1739 came to Mr. Wesley groaning for redemption, and asking advice as to how they were to flee from the wrath to come and be saved from their sins; nor the fact that their numbers increased daily. But we cannot follow the Wesleys, Whitefield, and their colaborers among the colliers, in the streets, in the woods, from a father's tombstone, everywhere preaching to the poor, while thousands receive the Word and are saved.

Let us glance at the planting of Methodism upon these Western shores. The Wesleys had preached in Savannah. Whitefield, like a burning comet, had crossed the Atlantic thirteen times, and preached from Georgia to New England. The revival in Great Britain had caught in almost every hamlet of the empire, and with nearly every colony of adventurers there were some of the members of their societies. These brought with them some of the fire and system of the revival from whence they came. Embury and Barbary Heck are immortal in New York; Strawbridge, in Maryland; Williams and King, borne on the tide of emigration to Virginia, fell the forest and support their families, yet go far and near preaching to the settlers, forming societies, building places of worship and breaking the fallow ground, preparing the field for the approaching harvest.

But time fails to enumerate the hosts of God's elect, who, from Maine to Georgia, prepared the fields before the missionaries arrived to take charge of them; as laymen planted Christianity of old in Antioch before the arrival of the first apostles.

Mr. Wesley sends over missionaries who find the fields "white unto the harvest." In 1773 the first Conference was held, and by 1776 the work had received body and form in nearly all the colonies. But the missionaries are Englishmen, and on the breaking out of the Revolutionary war most of them gave their influence with the mother country, and often "spoke unadvisedly with their lips." This resulted in the return of all the English missionaries, except the immortal Asbury. Yea, more, and worse: it fixed, as synonymous in the public mind the words "Methodist" and "Tory." A storm of persecution, unequaled in violence and extent, was waged against the now apparently helpless Church. But still they preached, and in 1776 new territory is invaded; in 1777 and 1778, amidst the shouts of battle and the fires of persecution, a revival is carried forward in Virginia and North Carolina, which adds eighteen hundred to their numbers.

We now pass to 1784. The storm of war is hushed, the colonies have become independent States. A General Conference is called to meet in Baltimore. The laborers assemble from all parts of the field. Here the Church is organized under the immortal Coke, the embodiment of missionary zeal, who laid wealth, honor, learning, and social position at the foot of the cross. Here the unity of order of bishop and elder is restored to apostolic usage, and the distinctive work of the former established. Here Asbury, who for thirteen years has labored as a missionary, is ordained bishop; who henceforth, without the aid of steam, is to travel his weary rounds annually from Maine to Georgia—preaching, presiding, ordaining, bearing the care of all the churches, for near half a century. Here the consecrated laborers, who, with no call but that of God, with no consecration but of the Holy Ghost, have planted and built up the Church—are now ordained, and henceforth are ministers not only of God, but also of the Church.

The little streams from their mountain homes have been united. Now swells the mighty river, which shall continue to flow, increasing in breadth, depth, and force until lost in eternity's mighty ocean.

II. THE PRESENT.

Let us now briefly survey the present. There were reported to the Ecumenical Council of Methodism, in 1881, thirty-two thousand six hundred and fifty-two itinerant preachers, eighty-nine thousand two hundred and ninety-two local preachers, and four million nine hundred and sixty-six thousand eight hundred and eighty-nine communicants, aggregating five million eighty-eight thousand eight hundred and thirty-three members, with five million three hundred and eighty-seven thousand nine hundred and eight officers, teachers, and pupils in our Sunday schools. With awe and wonder we exclaim: "What hath God wrought!"

And again we realize that God works through means. Hence the important question of this hour is: What have been the means so signally blessed during the last century? In answer we notice.

1. *Evangelical Doctrines.*—Here we make no apologies; nor do we at this time propose to offer any

proofs of the "correctness of our faith." The articles of our religion are embraced, more or less, by all evangelical branches of the Church. Those which are classed strictly Methodistic, we think, are clearly taught in the word of God, and, in the main, find a ready response in the human heart.

(1) We emphasize a salvation free and full, for every son and daughter of man. We believe that Christ so "tasted death for every man" as to make the salvation of each and every one possible, and that every soul lost is lost by voluntarily rejecting means within his reach for his salvation. This is the key-note which swells upon every breeze. To-day one hundred and twenty-one thousand nine hundred and forty-four Methodist preachers are urging this free and full salvation to over twenty millions of hearers.

(2) Again, as a distinctive doctrine, we preach the direct witness of the Spirit. Not only did Christ die for us all, but the Holy Ghost is ready to apply the blood and seal us heirs of heaven. Not only are we heirs, but it is also our privilege *now* to know whom we have believed and to experience what Paul describes when he exclaims: "For ye have not received the spirit of bondage again to fear; but ye have received the Spirit of adoption, whereby we cry, Abba, Father. The Spirit itself beareth witness with our spirit, that we are the children of God."

(3) We not only preach a free salvation, but a full salvation. Not only that each one may be saved, but fully saved; that the blood of Christ cleanseth from all sin; and the groaning after this perfect love gives intensiveness to all our efforts and is with us the chief source of all revival power.

(4) Again, we preach that man's probation closes with his life. Hence we offer salvation to the penitent thief, and promise a crown of life to the hoary-headed saint, upon condition of his being faithful until death.

2. *Compactness of Organization.*—Much of the success of our Church is due to the compactness of its organization.

(1) The itinerant system of ministerial labor, while it involves the mutual surrender of the minister in choosing his congregation, and of the congregation in choosing their pastor, secures to each minister a charge and to every congregation a pastor. It also secures those frequent changes which furnish variety to all. It furnishes a strong cavalry force, capable of concentration at every strategic point, and a vidette for every place, from the city full to the farthest point of the emigrant's camp. Thus we see a mighty host always in the saddle, with drawn sword, ready for the service of their Lord.

(2) The local preacher, without fee or reward, is ready to render service wherever needed. He aids in every revival, fills the pulpit of the pastor in his absence, seeks out places of destitution, and carries to the poor the bread of life. In the highways and hedges he calls for the poor, the maimed, the blind, and is ever found ready to fill any destitution in the itinerant ranks.

(3) Again, here is the exhorter, the class leader, the steward, the trustee, the Sunday school superintendent and teacher, the faithful and zealous layman, all at work—a place for every man and every man in his place. "All at it and all the time at it." This, at least, is the theory. God enable every one to fill

by active usefulness the place Providence has prepared for him!

(4) We may not pass this point without a remark upon woman's work in the Church. While we abhor effeminacy in man, or the assumption of manhood in woman, yet woman—"last at the cross and earliest at the grave"—has always occupied her place in the activities of the Church. The names of Mrs. Wesley, Mrs. Fletcher, Mrs. Rogers, and many others, are immortal in the rise of Methodism. From then till now the ranks of godly women crowd upon the canvas, and to-day—in the family circle, by the bed of the sick, in the class room, the missionary society, and temperance union—she adds wisdom, strength, and beauty to the temple of God. May their numbers increase a thousandfold!

3. *Spirituality.*—In noticing the present condition of the Church, with its elements of success, we have delayed noticing its spirituality until the present because we recognize this as the crowning glory of Methodism. While all believers in the Bible know that "God is a Spirit: and they that worship him must worship him in spirit and in truth," yet it is our chief glory that from the time Mr. Wesley "felt his heart strangely warmed" to the present, a spiritual regeneration, as well as justification by faith, has been the very life and soul of the Church. And here let us drop a word of caution to the ministry. Infidelity fears no man on the field of polemic strife. You may answer his sophistries, but he and the powers of hell only laugh and present another head for decapitation, while thousands of earth's sons and daughters are drifting to hell. But when God's min-

isters preach the word under the influence of the Holy Ghost and fire; when every minister cries to the Sanballats and Tobiahs, "I am doing a great work, . . . why should the work cease, whilst I leave it and come down to you?" then it is the chariot of God moves forward and the ranks of darkness hide from the face of truth. We cannot be too guarded here. We have education. God increase it a thousandfold! We have magnificent churches, and many appliances which our fathers had not. But we ask: Does the spiritual power of the Church increase with its material strength? If the day ever comes when learning, eloquence, and all fortuitous circumstances combined shall be admitted as a substitute for spirituality and spiritual preaching in the Church, then "*Mene, mene, tekel, upharsin*" will be written on the wall.

4. *Objects of These Services.*—We next notice the objects of these centennial services.

(1) Methodism was born in a revival. Indeed, the New Testament Church was ushered in amid the sound of a rushing, mighty wind, cloven tongues of fire, earnest, fervent preaching, conviction by the Spirit of God, repentance, salvation, and the adding of three thousand the first day, and afterwards God added to their numbers daily. This was not a revival that fell into the old grooves as soon as the protracted meeting was over. But the fire still burned, the preachers still preached, the Church still prayed, and God added new converts to their numbers daily. For seven days before the revival the disciples were all, with one accord, in one place praying for the baptism of the Holy Ghost. No wonder they had a revival,

no wonder their converts were numbered by thousands, and that their numbers increased. The same means were used in 1739. A few devout students fasted, prayed, and sought after holiness. God's Spirit aroused others; the valley of dry bones was shaken, and there stood up a great army. I love the pentecostal shout of thousands, where the Holy Ghost and fire rests upon the Church. I love the grand continued revival, where the Church is terribly in earnest, and the daily increase of the converts attests the work divine. Brethren, is the revival God's plan for the saving of humanity? Then why do we sleep while the souls of our people—souls bought with the blood of the Son of God, souls which must forever live—are drifting daily into hell? A revival in every congregation! Think of one hundred and twenty-one thousand ministers fasting and praying for a revival; think of one-fourth of a million congregations praying for a revival; think of five million members with one accord, at the mercy seat, praying for a revival; think of twenty million souls under our ministry, with the untold millions in the regions still beyond, all interested, all infinitely interested in a revival. Church of the living God! "I hear the tread of millions." The year is passing, a little revival power here and there, a few thousands added to the Church; but this is but the gentle mist portending the mighty rain; a slight tremor of the earth's surface, to be followed by the upheaval of mountains and continents. What can stand before the hosts of God's elect if we are in earnest, all with one accord in one place (at the mercy seat), and all speaking with tongues, as the Spirit gives utterance to the wonderful works of God? I may not live twenty years, but I do feel that before that time, if the whole Church were powerfully in earnest, the banner of the cross, decorated with the star of Bethlehem, would float from the ramparts of every city on the globe. The Hindoo and Caffre would send back the shout, swelling upon every breeze: "Alleluiah, the Lord God omnipotent reigneth!"

(2) The next point in our centennial services is a donation from every member of our congregation as a thank offering to Almighty God. Has he a right to our gratitude? We are his; he made us. We are his by redemption and preservation. From infancy till the present his right hand has upheld us. Our homes, our friends, wealth, honors, pleasures, Sabbaths, and Bibles, are all donations from his bountiful hand. And now he says to us: "Freely ye have received, freely give." "Go ye into all the world, and preach the gospel to every creature." Surrounded with ten thousand blessings from his hand, he calls upon us to-day for an offering of thanks. Not to God, as though he needed anything, but to Christ in the person of his poor. While we read our Bibles, enjoy his gospel with all the blessings of civil and religious liberty, millions of his creatures inhabit the dark places of earth and bow to stock and stone. If every member of our congregations could but realize our relation to God and to our common humanity, there would be spontaneous offerings sufficient to equip missionaries to every city of the globe. But we must aid them in building churches. No mission station is equpped until there is a house of prayer;

a place where God's name is recorded, and where his people meet to worship. And then our educational facilities must be increased. To-day, perhaps, thousands of young men feel the call of God upon them to preach, but they lack literary qualifications, and are too poor to obtain them. Church of God, come over and help them! In all our missionary operations the mission school is an essential part; while we preach to the adults, the children must be instructed. Men of Israel, help not with a nickel that you would throw to a beggar, but with an offering worthy of your God.

Let us now briefly glance at the entire subject. We have seen the little band in Oxford praying, working, and organizing until revival power wraps England with glory. We have accompanied the emigrant to America, and heard the shouts of salvation among the forests of the New World. We have looked in upon Embury in his sail loft in New York, and Strawbridge in Maryland, with hosts of heroes in Virginia, the Carolinas, and Georgia. We have seen the Church organizing in Baltimore; have accompanied Asbury in his ample rounds. We have moved down the stream while Jerry, Evans, Tally, and Slade were planting the standard in Florida. We have watched the pioneer felling the forest and preaching the cross from Maine to Florida, from the Atlantic to the Pacific. For one hundred years we have listened to the swelling notes of victory, while the number of converts has increased to millions. We have sought and found the secret source of power, and to-day we raise our Ebenezer, for hitherto the Lord hath helped us.

III. The Future.

Now a glance at the future, and then we close. When I first stood upon the banks of the Mississippi my first sensation was that of disappointment, then of awe as I contemplated the majesty of that mighty stream. Thought wandered away to the little stream far off in the regions of eternal ice. And from the snow-capped Alleghanies on the east to the inaccessible crags of the Rocky Mountains on the west, and down to the Gulf on the south, there is not a square inch of land that does not feel its force, and is not watered and drained by its secret springs.

Yea, through the Gulf, by the Antilles, around the reefs of Florida, by the coast of Labrador, and on across the ocean and upon the shores of the East its benign influence is still felt. God Almighty, speed on the stream of Methodism until every square inch of our sin-cursed earth shall feel its sacred influence; until every son and daughter of man shall join in the songs of the redeemed; until eternity's mighty ocean shall swell in loud alleluiahs to Him that hath loved us, and washed us in his own blood, to whom be glory, honor, praise, power, and salvation, now and forever! Amen.

A SERMON.*

"And now, brethren, I commend you to God, and to the word of his grace, which is able to build you up, and to give you an inheritance among all them which are sanctified." (Acts xx. 32.)

A MORE sublime character than St. Paul has never walked the strand of time, saving our Lord Jesus Christ. Born and raised in Tarsus, brought up at the feet of Gamaliel, a Hebrew of the Hebrews, by religion a Pharisee, touching the law blameless, in zeal for the faith of the fathers excelling all competitors. But when miraculously convicted and converted to Christianity, he laid learning, fame, and power at the foot of the cross. Conferring not with flesh and blood, he immediately began preaching the faith he had once destroyed.

He was now making his last journey to Jerusalem, where he knew that bonds and imprisonment awaited him. And from Miletus he sent to Ephesus and called for the elders of the Church. He had planted Christianity there, having for three years labored, preaching from house to house repentance toward God and faith in our Lord Jesus Christ; and now before him stood the representatives of the fruits of his ministry.

With a burning heart he warns them against the grievous wolves which should enter in; not sparing the flock, the apostates from among themselves, who

---

*Preached in McTyeire Memorial Church, Jacksonville, Fla., January 10, 1895, on the jubilee occasion of the fiftieth anniversary of the Florida Conference.

would draw away followers; and, rising to the sublime heights of the occasion, he cries: "And now, brethren, I commend you to God, and to the word of his grace, which is able to build you up, and to give you an inheritance among all them which are sanctified."

This subject has been selected beause of its appropriateness to our present service.

Fifty years have run their ample rounds since first I preached upon Florida's soil. Half a century has been numbered with the ages before the flood since the first roll call of the Florida Conference was borne away on the breeze, and now we meet to celebrate our first jubilee.

Your speaker does not recognize his selection for this important service as a result of any peculiar fitness on his part for the work, or for ability to fill the hour as acceptably as many others who sit before him, but simply to the fact that he stands alone upon the effective list of those who participated in the exercises of the Conference of 1845. And should he seem egotistical by frequent personal reference, it is only because he cannot otherwise so clearly present thoughts of interest.

In this relation I would try to lay one hand above the mighty dead and point to their labors, conflicts, and triumphs only as object lessons to those who follow; and I would lay the other hand upon the heads of the heroic living and commend them to God and the word of his grace.

"I commend you to God"—not to Apollos, Cephas, or John. Although he well knew that other apostles and preachers of gigantic minds and loving hearts would preach to them in the future, yet he commended his hearers not to them but to God. The apostles were itinerant preachers, and their method of rotating among the churches is the spirit of Methodism to-day. But neither he nor any other minister, in the sense of our text, would dare commend his flock to his successors, but to God, the eternity of whose existence, the infinity of whose power, whose omniscience and omnipresence present to our faith a being we can always trust; whose truth knows no change, and the very essence of whose existence is love; for "God is love." Here, my brother, you may safely lead and securely leave your flock. And while I would shout, "Harvest home!" over the triumphs of a jubilee, I would join the immortal Massillon, who, beholding the grand pageantry of the hour, and presence of the dead king, after three efforts to speak, each of which was choked by emotion, rose to his uttermost height, and with all the power of his voice cried: "There is nothing great but God!" And here let us pause to say that the men of power who labored in the past to bring our Conference to its present state were men who "walked with God," and whose lives, as well as their preaching, were a reflection of the divine image; men who went from their knees to the pulpit, and from the pulpit to the closet. They were princes who prevailed first with God and then with men.

"To the word of his grace." The word of his grace may refer to Christ, as in the benediction: "The grace of the Lord Jesus Christ." We all know that the grace of Christ is the sinner's only hope, and well might the apostle commend them to that grace. But while this may be one meaning of the text, we think it applies to the burning words of inspiration. Christ says: "Search the Scriptures; they testify of me." The Bible is the only rule of faith, and the guide to lead us to salvation here and glory hereafter. To be a successful minister a man must be "mighty in the Scriptures." The heroic dead were men who adopted Mr. Wesley's motto: "*Homo unus liber.*" They were emphatically men of one book. Who that ever heard John L. Jerry preach could ever forget his familiarity with the Book, especially with the Psalms? Peyton P. Smith, in the burning words of inspiration, while the Divine Spirit accompanied the word, so preached that the sinner felt himself trembling over the very flames of hell. But why need I multiply examples when the burden of every sermon was the Word of God? Paul was a philosopher, a prince of logicians, a poet, and an orator; but I hear him declare to those whom he had served: "I determined not to know anything among you save Jesus Christ and him crucified." One sermon drawn from the word of his grace is worth more than whole volumes combating the errors of science, falsely so called. The world is full of theories and the wildest theorists; men who claim fellowship with the "schools" announce hypotheses of creation, which rule God out of the universe and make man a little higher order of animal. But, my brethren, if such men can glory in tracing their ancestry back through the monkey, tadpole, and protoplasm, let them glory in their ignoble lineage. But, my brethren, ye are the offspring of the Lord Almighty, and do you preach the word of his grace.

The philosophy of our day may enlarge our intellectual facilities, the investigations of science may increase our knowledge; and these, if held in their proper places, may be a blessing to man. But nothing can build up the Church and raise men to a higher moral plane but God and the word of his grace. The religion of the Bible is divine. All the schools of morality, science, and philosophy are but menmade ladders upon which fools endeavor to climb to the skies. Until man can reach infinity by looping together things finite, there is no hope of salvation but in God and the word of his grace. And in illustration of this let us take a brief review of the past.

Go with me back to that little band that met in Tallahassee February 6, 1845. Before us stands the venerable Joshua Soule, the senior bishop of our Church, who, surveying our territory from Albany, Ga., and the Altamaha River to Key West, Fla., and from the Atlantic to Apalachicola, and seeing but thirty-three men to occupy the field, and about half of them untutored youths, he exclaims: "When I see your vast and sparsely settled territory, and the small number of preachers, I almost wish myself a young man and a member of the Florida Conference." But the field was manned as best it could be. At that day there at least seemed to be no seeking of place among the preachers, and no seeking of men among the laity, but looking to God we prayed, believed, and worked, as receiving our appointments from him. The Conference work accomplished, our appointments announced, we shake hands and start east, west, north, and south, singing our parting hymn:

> The vineyard of the Lord
> Before his lab'rers lies;
> And lo! we see the vast reward
> That waits us in the skies.

But what was the character of that vineyard, and what the nature of the laborers' work? The seven years' Indian war had just closed, and farmers were returning to their desolate homes. In East Florida, while a few planters were opening large plantations, their families were generally left behind.

The large majority of our population were range men who came to Florida for the benefit of their flocks. These settled in groups of five to twenty-five, for mutual protection from wild beasts and savage Indians. From one of these groups to the other there would probably be five, ten, twenty, and even forty miles. The missionary generally preached every day in the week, carrying his pocket compass. Striking a given course, he would travel so many miles, perhaps fall into an Indian trail and follow it to the settlements, where the neighbors gathered and heard him preach in one of the houses of the settlement. The men generally carried their rifles to church and stacked them in the corner till preaching was over. This was done for protection, should a band of Indians attack them, and for the further purpose of killing a deer or two after preaching was over.

As to roads, at that day we had the King's Highway, from St. Augustine to St. Mary's River, via Cowford (now Jacksonville); the Bellamy road, from Tallahassee to St. Augustine; the Government road, from the Georgia line to Tampa Bay; and a few shorter ones cut by the troops during the war. As to bridges, none. As to ferries, we had some two or three upon the St. John's, and three upon the Suwannee. The small rivers and creeks we swam. Sometimes a settler would have a dugout and carry the missionary over, while his horse would swim by its side; but generally he would be alone, and his horse was his only canoe. I have known a preacher to swim three streams in the morning before reaching his appointement, preach, ride a number of miles in the afternoon, and sleep in his wet clothes at night.

I cannot leave this part of the subject without a word of commendation to the kind pioneers of East Florida at that day. There was nothing in their power too good for God's ministers. The best they could command they set before him; and would often walk miles, wading through the water, for their preacher to walk across a swollen stream upon a fallen log, then take his horse and swim it over, and, meeting the parson on the other shore, would shake his hand and send him dry to his next appointment.

The first band of laborers soon began to pass away. Two years, and R. A. Griffin answered not to roll call; five years, and Alexander Martin was not with us; and to-day only Dr. Blake and your speaker answer to the roll call of those who took appointments then, and if any others live except G. W. Pratt, of Palatka, and the unique Simon Peter Richardson, of the North Georgia Conference, I know it not. But before the first passed away others came in, and from year to year our members increased, and at almost every Conference our line was a little longer, and the fields a little broader.

In 1866 we lost nearly half of our territory, and nearly half of our preachers, when the South Georgia Conference was formed. But this was soon made up, and we are still increasing, till to-day, though our Conference does not cover so much territory as two districts did at first, we mount the ramparts with one hundred and thirty-seven men. Nailing our banner to the outer wall, we shout defiance to earth and hell, crying: "What hath God wrought!"

Now, my brother, are not God and the word of his grace able to build us up? As far as I know, after the organization of our Conference, the first house of prayer was erected under my ministry—a small log house at Fort Call, with hewn puncheon floor and seats. It was a rude building, but it answered the wants of the people there in 1845. Little did we then think of the nucleus of power then planted, nor that in after years it should be said in triumph that this or that man was born there. But now I see churches almost everywhere, and many of them magnificent structures. In 1846 I called together the few members we had in Tampa—seventeen in number—in a small house belonging to the United States garrison, and organized them into a church. I now look at their magnificent building, their numbers and wealth, thank God, and take courage. I remember in 1850 organizing a little band of about fifteen persons into a church in Palatka, in an old government building. As I look at the present state of that church, and think of its members who have already crossed the flood in peace, I raise my hands in triumph, crying: "What hath God wrought!"

The same year I drew the titles for a piece of land

in Ocala. At that time we worshiped in a small log house which served for courthouse, theater, dancing hall, lecture room and church. To-day I see upon that land one of the most beautiful churches in our State, surrounded by one of the most pleasant pastoral charges.

In 1851-52 I served the Jacksonville Station. This city, without reproach, might have been called a village. It was a single man's station. I think of those two years as among the happiest of my itineracy. We more than doubled our membership, raised the money, repaired and painted our little chapel. That chapel, years afterwards, gave way to St. Paul's, and that, as the years rolled on, to McTyeire Memorial Church, upon the ground where we now worship.

But the fathers, where are they? There may be no vacant places at this communion chancel, but they are not filled by those to whom I broke the bread and to whom I gave the cup in 1852. "God takes away his workmen, but carries on his work." As sad memories of the past mingle with august surroundings of the present, and still more glorious hopes for the future, in triumph we shout: "Alleluiah, the Lord God omnipotent reigneth." But let us not rest in material success, and recline at ease under the shadow of turreted cathedrals and minarets of wealth. No Church can rise higher than the aggregate Christian character of its members, nor become broader than the purity of those called by its name. Every person saved from sin adds one polished stone to God's glorious temple, but not every name added to the register, nor every dollar cast into the treasury of the Church, adds to its success or power. God and the word of his grace must do the work, and unadulterated Christian character is the only material we can use in its construction. Sanctified education, refinement, and eloquence may all be used to profit in preparing the material, but God and his word must build the temple. I see before me, in imagination, to-night, the venerable John Slade, one of our oldest pioneers, tall, slender, upright, his face burning like a comet, silver locks covering his head. With a voice grating harsh thunder he points the sinner to his doom, and with streaming eyes, while a halo of glory brightens his face, points the Christian to the pearly gates, the golden streets, and crystal river of the city of God, and whole congregations moved as the golden grain bows before the breeze. O brother, when God uses the minister, and the word of his grace is the theme, the Church will rise and saints will shout for joy.

"And to give you an inheritance among all them which are sanctified." The doctrine of sanctification is not only scriptural, but it is Methodistic. Although I have heard that there are whole shiploads of Methodist preachers in this country who are opposed to sanctification, I thank the Lord that I have never met one of them. Although I may not believe every word that everybody says about sanctification, yet the doctrine I believe with all my heart, and I have preached it more than half a century. We all know that the sanctified soul is set apart from the service of the world, the flesh, and the devil, to love and serve God. We know that perfect love casteth out fear; that we may have "peace as a river and righteousness as the waves of the sea;" that we may love the Lord with all the heart, the soul, the mind, and strength, and our neighbor as ourselves; that we may do to others as we would have them do to us. We know that our good is all divine; that whatsoever good is in us is wrought by the Holy Ghost through the merits of Christ and received by faith. Then let us all quit disputing about the mere drapery, and preach and live the divine doctrine, knowing that our inheritance is among the sanctified.

"To give you an inheritance"—one that will give you access to the best society in the universe. The friends and companions of kings and queens may count themselves honored, but our inheritance gives us a place among the sons and daughters of the King of kings; yea, enables us truthfully to say to him, "My Father," in whose presence all kings and queens are less than grasshoppers.

I see a man, poor, afflicted, and despised; but a holy calm rests upon his brow, peace is the girdle of his loins. Who is he? An heir of God, with the promise of an "inheritance incorruptible, undefiled, and that fadeth not away."

www.ingramcontent.com/pod-product-compliance
Lightning Source LLC
Chambersburg PA
CBHW071609170426
43196CB00034B/2245